ALL THE PAINTINGS OF
LEONARDO DA VINCI

VOLUME TWO
in the
Complete Library of World Art

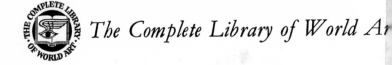

The Complete Library of World Ar

ALL THE PAINTINGS OF

LEONARDO DA VINCI

Text by COSTANTINO BARONI

Translated from the Italian by
PAUL COLACICCHI

HAWTHORN BOOKS, INC.

Publishers · New York

Printed in Great Britain by
Jarrold and Sons, Ltd, Norwich

CONTENTS

LEONARDO DA VINCI

His life and his art

LEONARDO'S fame as a universal genius has earned him the reputation of being the most perfect expression of the "Ideal Man of the Renaissance". In other words, he responded in full to the whole complex of creative impulses engendered by Humanism and at the same time was deeply moved by a thirst for scientific knowledge of the world as a prelude to his development of individual research based on experimental method. In some ways the importance of his scientific achievements has tended to obscure the profound nature of his towering accomplishments in the arts.

While, on one hand, few would dispute his supremacy as a subtle catalyst of Renaissance artistic thought—one of the most lofty and complete in the history of civilization—the fact remains that opinion of Leonardo the artist is still enclosed in a kind of myth. Since the content of his painting cannot be fully explained in psychological terms nor in terms of reason alone, his critics have often concluded their studies by emphasizing the extraordinary scientific objectives and accomplishments of Leonardo and have used these to compensate for the scarcity of surviving finished painting by the Master and justifying the scarcity by acknowledging that certain paintings of great significance were allowed to remain unfinished and that an unknown number of others deteriorated because they were executed with experimental techniques developed by the Master which proved impermanent and so are lost to us.

The mistake, in this case, has been to consider that Leonardo's prime purpose in painting was to produce a series of finished works. Actually he employed his great artistic skill to record in some degree the poetic imagery which hung suspended in his mind and which the hand of even this man could not fully express through physical means. In fact, Leonardo used to remark, "When our thinking soars beyond the limits of the hand, this is a most desirable condition." He implies that speculation may advance with a kind of chain reaction and lead to conclusions and achievements of special significance not directly connected with the initial assignment. Living in a world marked by sharp tension, swift transition, and heightened creative movement, he admonishes the true thinker not to boast of knowing the laws of nature but to find satisfaction in understanding the new things he invents within his own mind.

The artist was born out of wedlock to Ser Piero, a notary of Florence, and a mother of humble station, in Vinci in 1452. Although he did not like to talk about his childhood it haunted his memory. As a young man he was thoughtful, unstable, eager to learn; he was pleasant and graceful; his language was affable, his vocabulary so rich that it sometimes surprised even himself. Most of all, he impressed people with his intelligence and the ease with which he could learn.

At seventeen he was sent by his father to study painting under Verrocchio, in whose workshop he quickly proved himself a master. Many distinguished men gathered there, and young Leonardo would hear them talking on a variety of subjects: painting, the mechanical arts, philosophy, and new technical discoveries.

Everything seemed to fascinate him, and he was constantly experimenting in a multitude of different directions. His restlessness appeared to some as the sign of an irregular life. This happened in 1476 when he had been for over five years a member of the Company of Florentine Artists and had already produced that outstanding drawing (now in the Uffizi Gallery) of a landscape of hills rolling down to the plain, which Berenson described as "of a touch so delicate, almost Japanese". He had written on one side of this work: "Sancta Maria della Neve, August 2, 1473."* There is already in this drawing much of the pictorial and graphic quality that was to make da Vinci as great a draughtsman as Pisanello, Dürer, or Rembrandt His line is never merely descriptive, but rather interconnected with the substance of his subject, and at the same time intensely autobiographical —in other words, closely related to the emotional moment which his hand is recording. In the subtle vibration of an open, luminous atmosphere we find an energy of movement, extended even to the rocks and trees, which appeared to satisfy the aspirations of half a century of Florentine painting, from Masaccio to Antonio Pollaiuolo, in so far as it reconnected the wilfulness of the Humanistic myth to a motherly nature.

In the *Baptism of Christ*, *circa* 1475, now at the Uffizi (plate 1), Verrocchio allowed his pupil a free hand in painting the angel kneeling on the left with drapery over the right arm. This is the first positive sign that Leonardo had achieved the full development of his means of expression. Part of the landscape is also attributed to him. In this painting the energy of the figures, typical of Verrocchio, seems to dissolve in the limpid, pearl-like surfaces and in the fluid transparency of the atmosphere which, though richly

* For other critics the date is August 5. (Translator's note.)

luminous, is replete with molecular vibrations receding from the clear-cut figures to the impending dusk enveloping the distant hills. This effect gives to the whole picture a sense of grace and spirituality and adds a fresher emotional quality to the harmony of lines previously achieved by Rossellino, Filippo Lippi, and Botticelli. But at the same time the construction of the whole picture reflects order, intellectual clarity, and free-flowing rhythm—all elements in the purest Tuscan tradition.

It is unthinkable that the earlier collaboration between Verrocchio and Leonardo was continued in the painting of the *Annunciation*, in the Uffizi. Angelico, Filippo Lippi, and Verrocchio had all reverted to the "ancient simplicity" of Donatello, while here a palpitating light appears to caress the beautiful shapes of the Virgin and Angel, haloed by a tremulous chiaroscuro—a foretaste of the visual magic of da Vinci's *sfumato*.

In the interval between these pictures it is clear that Leonardo had begun working independently. He once stated that "poor is the pupil who does not surpass his master". As a consequence he taught that no artist can hope to excel if he is merely content to copy others. He will have to learn from nature, as did the great artists, from Giotto to Masaccio: he who followed these teachings became "a nephew of Nature and a kinsman of God".

It is therefore necessary to acquire a personal experience of the world and then, by use of the imagination, to invent a wider world of thought. Through that "mental discourse" which is painting, man may acquire a complete knowledge of himself and satisfy his natural thirst for information. In young Leonardo every extrinsic application of knowledge to experimental science, in its theoretical or practical directions, is always ultimately brought back to an all-embracing figurative poetry and is therefore filled with elusive meaning, obscure symbolism, and metaphoric allusion. For instance, the sensitively colored bust of so-called *Ginevra de' Benci*, in the Liechtenstein Gallery (color plate II), painted about 1478, recalls the languid grace of a flower growing in the shadow of juniper trees and reflecting the last rays of sunlight upon the water. But there is contained here a restless pyschological vitality which leaves the impression of something not fully expressed, something beyond the mere text of the picture, something that will later be realized in the supreme enchantment of the *Mona Lisa* (plate 62).

At this period Leonardo also evolved a series of fanciful and brilliant variations on the iconic theme of the Virgin. In September 1478, Leonardo wrote: "I have started to paint the two Marys." This subject, in the painting of which the Florentines had achieved a maximum of poetic feeling and gentleness (thanks to a particular melodious line which left her features as pure as those of a medallion profile) was presented by da Vinci on an entirely new emotional and formal basis. In the *Madonna with vase of flowers* (plate 5), now in the Munich Pinakothek, the contrast between the interior darkness, creating an intimate atmosphere, and the glittering light of the Alpine landscape seen through the mullioned window, resolves itself in the static thoughtfulness of the divine group; the marble-like quality of the drapery emerging from the shadows in three colors, light blue, ruby, and golden-yellow, the flowers on the right, the crystal vase, and the ivory tonality of the chubby infant's flesh—all these contribute to the general effect of a cold refraction of light very similar to that of the distant mountain peaks.

Look, instead, at the *Madonna of the Flower*, or the Benois *Madonna*, in the Leningrad Hermitage (plate 4). Here the sudden impressionistic gesture of the Child grasping his Mother's hand shows us an artist who is translating the energetic linearity of Antonio Pollaiuolo and Botticelli into a freer expression of movement, thereby creating an effect which involves our whole field of vision. Finally, look at the nursing *Madonna Litta* (plate 74) only traditionally attributed to Leonardo: here the whole is subtly organized into a balance of pure rhythm and lyrical movement.

That the public soon began to appreciate Leonardo's paintings is proved by the fact that in 1478 he received a commission from the Signoria (governing body) of Florence to paint a panel for the Chapel of San Bernardo in the Palazzo Vecchio. This work, together with many others, has unfortunately been lost, and nothing of them remains except an occasional—and often ambiguous—mention, or a reflection in the Master's drawings.

Three years later, in 1481, the monks of San Donato a Scopeto commissioned from Leonardo a complicated altar-piece, with the *Adoration of the Magi*, the preparatory panel for which is now in the Uffizi (plate 18).

The painting was never completed. The wood panel shows only a monochrome sketch; it is, however, fascinating for the earthy quality of its austere umber brown and olive-green mixture which was, in fact, the basic chromatic register of the chiaroscuro method, rigidly employed by the Tuscans. The composition is a richly involved one, the episodes being compactly grouped in such a way as to impart new tension and animation to the old narrative composition of Masaccio, such as may be seen in the *Baptism of the Neophytes* in the Brancacci Chapel, Florence. There is, at the same time, in the intense facial characterizations, in the excited mimicry of the figures, and in the whole choreography of the picture, the beginnings of a sublime language which will be used, a quarter of a century later, by Raphael in the Vatican *Stanze* and by Michelangelo in the Sistine Chapel. Observe, in Leonardo's *Adoration* the powerfully evocative scenery in the background above the figures, half-archaeological and half-wild, reminding one of the Elysian visions of Petrarch.

The same considerations of time and style should, presumably, apply to another monochrome preparation for a *St Jerome*, now in the Vatican Gallery (plate 24). Here, however, the picture is more markedly plastic and precise, the style rather more academic. This is an unfinished work, due to circumstances rather than intention. Leonardo unexpectedly decided to leave Florence. He must have been hoping for time to find elsewhere, in a more hospitable and less competitive city, the ease and means he needed in order to have an outlet for his inventive faculties. In a well-known letter of application to Ludovico Sforza, ruler of Milan, written about 1482, da Vinci stated that, besides being known as an artist, he was also exceptionally gifted as a civil and military engineer, and expert in the fields of architecture and hydraulics. He was eager to find employment there and to plunge into further studies.

Milan offered him a series of challenging opportunities, such as the project for an equestrian monument in honor of Francesco Sforza, plans for the improvement of the city's lay-out and for a new system of navigable waterways between the rivers Adda and Ticino; and other difficult architectural problems, such as the central dome of the Duomo. Later he was asked to organize celebrations and choreographical processions, and to execute pictorial decorations for many of the ducal residences.

In Milan and the University town of Pavia, where he was called to give architectural advice on the cathedral,

Leonardo met other noted artists and humanists, among them Bramante and Francesco di Giorgio. Yet in spite of his scientific accomplishments, he found that his time was most in demand as a painter. The first task he was given when he arrived in Milan was the painting of an altarpiece for the Chapel of the Confraternita della Concezione in the Church of San Francesco, with the assistance of the Milanese brothers, Ambrogio and Evangelista De Predis. This work, commissioned to be delivered not later than December 8, 1483, became the famous *Virgin of the Rocks* of which two versions now exist: one, entirely by Leonardo, is in the Louvre (plate 26) and the other, to which the Master contributed very little, is in London's National Gallery (plate 27). The situation here is complicated by the certainty that only the latter panel has been identified as part of the Milan altarpiece. It was delivered to the monks of the Brotherhood only in 1486, a fact that caused litigation which was carried on into the following century. In the case of both pictures the effective priority of the *Virgin of the Rocks*, in terms of time, over all the other paintings by Leonardo during the first part of his stay in Milan, is extremely controversial. The picture recalls the theme of St Jerome's dark cave in the *St Jerome* in the Vatican Gallery. It should be noted that Leonardo had now found a new and subtle way of imparting a tender sadness to his beautiful faces: these emerge slowly, one by one, from the deep mystery of the background into the light, acquiring a crystal-like smoothness and clarity. They are an amiable, quietly conversing group, these creatures from another world, and yet they radiate innocence and purity. The enchanting Flemish realism of the vegetation, as well as the clarity of the figures' gestures and signs, do not affect in the least the higher plane of intelligence that lends a richer spirituality to the Virgin and the Angel. These

14

two figures belong to the same noble cast as another painting which is tentatively attributed to Leonardo, the *Lady with an Ermine*, dated about 1490 in the Czartoryski Museum, Cracow (plate 76).

Leonardo was now about to embark on the perilous venture of the *The Last Supper*, in Santa Maria delle Grazie, a masterpiece hailed by his contemporary, Sabba da Castiglione, as "a work certainly divine, and famous all over the world" (plates 40–41).

How da Vinci envisaged this majestic creation; how he made it harmonize with the physical space allowed it in the refectory and with the particular conditions of light; how he attempted to find the models who could most suitably sit for his powerful cast of participants; the damage to his reputation caused by the idle gossip about this great work; and finally the lamentations that greeted his short-lived pigments—because he had ill-advisedly used the tempera instead of the fresco technique; anyone can discover these facts by studying his drawings and reading the literary references relating to the painting. But should one want to understand the text, as it were, of the picture—a difficult task because of the injuries of time and unskilled repairs—one must keep in mind that the narrative tissue, psychologically emphasized, is not the only reason for the pictorial importance of *The Last Supper*; in fact it is there to add a more touching accent of truth to an extremely dramatic moment which the Master was able to describe in a composed and calm architectonic form. The scheme was probably suggested by a previous work by Andrea del Castagno, but here the whole monumental structure achieves an effortless ease and plausibility, thereby entitling us to compare da Vinci's work to the heroic serenity of the Parthenon sculpture. An epic quality has been achieved by Leonardo through seemingly simple means. The intricate embellishments of lunettes and vault-ings, immediately above the main painting, were not due to a desire for dramatic effect. Thanks to those embellishments, on the one hand, the Apostles' figures emerge in a better plastic light; on the other hand that very wave of animated participation which we admire in the picture is contained and commensurated inside one structural register. The sequence of movement and action are important not so much for the life that they impart to this or that Apostle, but as a dynamic principle.

Grouped three by three in triangular patterns, the Apostles do not have their names written underneath (as Ghirlandaio and Andrea del Castagno had done), but are clearly recognizable by their facial traits, corresponding to the specific character of each as conveyed in the Scriptures. In the center Christ is silhouetted against the sky framed by the open door, his only halo being the evening light. Before his bent head Judas draws back, clenching his hands and overturning the salt, horrified at what he has done. The Giottoesque contrast between the two is here rendered by the light: Jesus is illumined with it; Judas is totally immersed in shadow.

The tremendous significance of the subject might in fact have overwhelmed da Vinci to the point where he dared not use the fresco technique—which requires speed and an almost spontaneous execution—and led him to work in tempera instead, perhaps including some new experimental ingredients which did not long hold firmly to the plaster ground, nor that to the wall.

This masterpiece excels all other works, paintings, and sculpture carried out by him in the first period of his stay in Milan. Most of these works have been lost, the attribution of others remains controversial, but they were completed, if at all, in the midst of scientific and literary research, of philosophical meditations, and protracted periods of travel throughout Italy.

Leonardo was now recognized and honored in the Court of the Sforzas and elsewhere as one of the most remarkable men of his century. He no longer suffered from financial worries. As he planned more and greater accomplishments for the glory of the dukedom, a group of his disciples, which included such men as De Predis, Boltraffio, and Salai, was gradually instilling in the public a taste for the "Leonardesque manner" which, being the product of a refined society, opposed to the Lombards' austere simplicity a cultured and languid beauty, a beauty both subtle and idealistic.

The years between 1485 and 1495 were, for Leonardo, intense, almost happy years. His features had become noble and grave; he was known as a sage, though perhaps somewhat eccentric and solitary. His are the words: "If you are alone you belong entirely to yourself." In him, as La Fontaine said, *"Tout était bonheur, jusqu'au sombre plaisir d'un cœur mélancolique."* And all the while he was contemplating colossal feats: the building of new bridges and military machines; the organization, for the Court, of fountain displays, tournaments, and theatrical spectacles; the erection of shooting-lodges. He was disputed over by the cream of the nobility and scientific circles. Yet at the end of the century da Vinci was to see the collapse of all his dreams based upon the ambitious Sforza's reign and to see French troops occupying Milan. He stayed briefly in Mantua where he made a fine chalk drawing of Isabella d'Este (plate 56), the cartoon of which, now in the Louvre, he took with him to Venice where it was admired by Lorenzo da Pavia for its resemblance to the original. A short time later he was sent by the Signoria of Venice to study the fortifications of the River Isonzo, but at the end of April 1500, he was back in Florence, probably intending to remain there for some time. He took up his beloved studies once again and undertook, for the Servite Brothers of Annunziata, an altarpiece of great importance: *St Anne, Virgin and Child*, a cartoon for which (plate 57) is now in London at Burlington House.

This drawing achieves such a high aesthetic realization that it ranks as a masterpiece itself. It is endowed with a greater concentration of plastic reality than the later panel in the Louvre (plate 66). The Burlington House cartoon, however, cannot be the one Vasari describes as shown to the public in Florence with such success that "for two days there was a constant procession of men and women going to see it, as people go to a solemn feast" (see remarks on plate 57).

While once again Leonardo enjoyed fame and popularity in Florence, he still maintained widespread associations. In Mantua, Isabella continued for many years to write to the Master expressing admiration; in Ferrara the Duke, and in Paris, the King's favorite, Robertet, were competing for the few paintings that, after many requests, da Vinci chose to finish. People complained that his "mathematical experiments have so diverted him from painting that he cannot endure his brushes". Da Vinci wanted nothing better than to be left to his beloved scientific studies and philosophical meditations. Nevertheless he welcomed, in 1503, his appointment as Architect and Chief Engineer to Duke Cesare Borgia, a position which took him over a great part of Central Italy to plan and direct canal and harbor constructions, as well as military works. Shortly after this, the Florentine Signoria recalled him, wishing to avail themselves of his assistance in the war against Pisa (Leonardo, in this case, planned nothing less than a deviation of the course of the River Arno!) and later to consult him on many artistic questions. Finally, in 1504, he undertook to compete with Michelangelo for the two great battle-scenes on the walls of the new Council Hall in the Palazzo Vecchio. What happened in this instance is generally well known. While Michelangelo, disdaining any exact historical reference, prepared innumerable muscular studies for a scene of the Florentine forces surprised in the act of bathing near Pisa, Leonardo chose as his subject the Battle of Anghiari (plates 86–88), an episode in the victory won by the Florentines in 1440 over Niccolò Piccinino. The episode represents the tremendous struggle for the colors between the opposing sides; Leonardo da Vinci meditated carefully on every subject before committing it to canvas. This is what he has to say about the "Way to represent a battle".

"As for the combatants, the more they are in the midst of this turmoil the less they will be visible and the less will be the contrast between their highlights and shadows.

"You should give a ruddy glow to the faces and figures and the air around them. The figures which are between you and light, if far away will appear dark against a light background, and the nearer their limbs are to the ground the less they will be visible, for there the dust is greater and thicker.

"Make the conquered pallid, with brows raised and knit together, and let the skin upon the brows be full of lines of pain; at the sides of the nose show the furrows going in an arch from the nostrils and ending where the eye begins, and show the dilation of the nostrils which is the cause of these lines; and let the lips be arched, displaying the upper row of teeth, and let the teeth be parted after the manner of such as cry in lamentation."

The Battle of Anghiari is a choral event, painted at the

height of battle, when the shrieking bodies are hurled one against the other and the sky is streaked with crimson flashes. A calculated concentration of plastic effects is evident in the many preparatory studies which the Master drafted, especially for the central theme of the fight for the colors. All that remain of the final composition are copies —including one by Rubens in the Louvre—for again the ill-advised choice of the "encausto" technique (a method by which the colors, whether tempera or some other kind remains in doubt, were to be laid on a specially prepared ground, and then both colors and ground made secure upon the wall by the application of heat) took effect unequally and the result was more or less complete failure. This induced da Vinci to desert a contest which since Michelangelo had already withdrawn, was now deprived of all competitive interest.

Offsetting this failure was the appearance at just this time of a unique masterpiece of figurative poetry, the *Mona Lisa*, in the Louvre (plate 62). We no longer seek the identity of the model, as the painting's reality is not biographical but psychological and moral. The posture of the seated young woman recalls the cartoon portraying Isabella d'Este. The enigmatic smile, reflecting the eternal secret of feminity has caused endless critical rhapsodies. And yet, as Walter Pater wrote: "Hers is the head upon which all 'the ends of the world are come'. It is beauty wrought out from within the flesh, the deposit, little cell by cell, of strange thoughts and fantastic reveries and exquisite passions. Set it for a moment beside one of those white Greek goddesses of beautiful women of antiquity, and how would they be troubled by this beauty, into which the soul with all its maladies has passed!"

And the background—the lazy, sinuous, meandering

river, in the evening shadows of a moonlit landscape—increases the dreamlike quality of the picture and transforms a portrait into an ideal vision. This is perhaps the secret of true art: to proceed from *real* objects toward an *ideal* subject.

Sensing the special quality of this work Leonardo refused to repeat this unique performance, as his numerous patrons would have him do. Neither could he rest upon his laurels. In 1506 he returned to Milan, called there by Charles d'Amboise, Maréchal de Chaumont, Lieutenant of the French King in Lombardy, a man of the world and a connoisseur of art. The Florence Signoria allowed da Vinci only three months leave of absence, but eventually an amicable agreement was reached transferring the Master's services to the King of France. Family matters, however, compelled him to visit Florence often in the following years, while he yearned for his home and vineyard in San Vittore, near Milan. Besides the paintings he had undertaken for King Louis, he carried on his researches in the fields of mechanics, anatomy, and hydraulics.

It is possible that this active and agreeable period of his life (around 1510) coincided with the new use of oils in *St Anne, Virgin and Child*, the subject of the London cartoon. This painting (plate 66) is now at the Louvre. In it the original idyllic theme acquires a new universal significance, due in part to the immense, luminous landscape which seems to reflect the vitality of the sinuous central group. Here Leonardo departed from the cartoon by stressing the pyramidal construction of the group. All his fundamental principles appear in this picture: the triangular composition, the nebulous background, the *sfumato* of the chiaroscuro, the expression of the faces, half-languid and half-mischievous. From da Vinci's *sfumato* all future painting was to move.

The word, in Italian, means "smoky". In this particular connexion it refers to the indistinct quality of the outlines. Leonardo painted his air as a fluid, into which he immersed his forms so that their outlines would fade like smoke and chiaroscuro would become an unnoticed passage from light to shadow. He wrote: "Notice in the streets at the fall of evening the faces of the men and women when it is bad weather; what grace and softness they display! When you wish to paint a portrait paint it in bad weather, at the fall of evening, and place the sitter with his back to one of the walls of the courtyard."

On September 24, 1513, Leonardo left for Rome with his pupils Melzi, Salai, and Fanfoia. This time the invitation had come from Giuliano de' Medici, the Pope's youngest brother, who gave him rooms in the Vatican's Belvedere for his scientific studies.

From Rome, still in the wake of Giuliano de' Medici and Pope Leo X, he went to Bologna, and hence to Florence, to be consulted about military and artistic problems of great relevance to the future of Italy. When, in 1516, Giuliano died, Leonardo had no patron, and although old and wise, he did not hesitate to embark on his last adventure. That most courteous of French kings, Francis I, not only showed him lavish hospitality but put at his disposal all the means that his Kingdom could make available for the daring feats of engineering that his inexhaustible mind was still conceiving.

The Master crossed the Alps with his faithful Melzi and one servant. He took with him his favorite paintings, from which he could not bear to be parted: *Mona Lisa*, *St Anne*, the swarthy *St John the Baptist* (plate 72), which are all now in the Louvre, and some panels, drawings, and manuscripts. He found lodgings in the Castle of Cloux, near Amboise, where in October 1517, he was visited by Cardinal Louis of Aragon. But the genius from Florence was tiring: paralysis had struck the Master's right hand, so that "nothing good could be expected" from him any more. And still he drafted and taught others to draw. His last message to the world, in his last will and testament, written at Cloux on April 23, 1519, shows that he gave himself to the Christian faith; he died on May 2, 1519, and was buried on August 12 in the cloister of Saint Florentin in Amboise. He had prepared himself for death with the dignity of an ancient sage, writing in his *Codice Atlantico*: "While I thought that I was learning to live, I have been learning how to die."

BIOGRAPHICAL NOTES

1452, APRIL 15. Leonardo is born in Anchiano, near the village of Vinci, the illegitimate son of Ser Piero da Vinci and Caterina di Piero del Vacca.

1469. The family moves to Florence. Leonardo is apprenticed in Verrocchio's workshop.

1470. He is enrolled in the lists of the Painters' Guild at Florence.

1478. He receives a commission for an altarpiece for the Chapel of St Bernard in the Palazzo della Signoria.

1481. The monks of the Convent of San Donato a Scopeto, in the suburbs of Florence, commission an altarpiece for their church.

1482. In a letter to the Duke of Milan, Leonardo offers his services as an engineer and an artist. The letter is recorded in the *Codice Atlantico*.

1483. In Milan, Leonardo da Vinci and the De Predis brothers sign a contract with the Brotherhood of the Conception of St Francis for an altarpiece divided into many panels, some of which were to be painted, others carved. (*The Virgin of the Rocks*.)

1485. Ludovico il Moro, Duke of Milan, commissions a panel to be sent as a present to Mathias Corvinus, King of Hungary.

1487–1490. He plans for the Cathedral's central dome and builds a wooden model illustrating his proposals.

1490, JANUARY 13. In the great Sforza stronghold, the Castello, a spectacular masquerade, the *Festa del Paradiso*, takes place. The settings and costumes are by Leonardo.

1490, JUNE 21. Leonardo is in Pavia, with Francesco di Giorgio and Amadeo. They are being consulted on the projected Cathedral of that city.

1491. Leonardo is pageant-master for Galeazzo Sanseverino, in the celebrations for the wedding of Ludovico Sforza with Beatrice d'Este.

1492. He is reported to be in Rome.

1494. He works near Vigevano, then visits the mining areas around Brescia.

1495. Leonardo, Michelangelo, Giuliano da San Gallo, Baccio d'Agnolo, and Cronaca, are called to Florence for consultations about the Great Council Hall in the Signoria Palace.

1495–1497. Leonardo is busily engaged in painting *The Last Supper* in the refectory of the Convent Church of Santa Maria delle Grazie, Milan. Some documents of the summer of 1497 (a letter by Ludovico il Moro to Marchesino Stanga, and the Master Book of Ducal Expenses) prove that the painting was not completed at that time.

1498. Leonardo is in Genoa, with other followers of the Duke. He decorates the Sala delle Asse and the Saletta Negra in Milan's Castello Sforzesco. Cecilia Gallerani sends to Isabella d'Este, at the latter's request, her portrait painted by Leonardo.

1499. Back in Florence and interested in physical geography, he expresses his views on the movements of the San Miniato hill.

1500. He passes through Venice: during a brief stay in Mantua he does a chalk drawing of Isabella d'Este. In April he passes through Florence.

1502. He is appointed Engineer General to Duke Cesare Borgia and inspects the latter's fortresses in the Romagna area.

1503. The Florentine Signoria orders from Leonardo a painting of the Battle of Anghiari for one of the two main walls of the Palazzo Vecchio's Council Hall.

1504. Leonardo takes part in a conference of artists to discuss the emplacement of Michelangelo's *David* in Florence.

1506. Maréchal Charles d'Amboise writes to the Florentine Signoria asking them to extend Leonardo's leave so that he may work in Milan.

1507. The King of France writes to the Signoria asking for an extension of Leonardo's leave.

1508. In the house of Diego Martelli, in Florence, Leonardo starts on a new book of notes. In September he is back in Milan pursuing hydraulic matters.

1513. He leaves Milan for Rome, where he is given lodgings in the Vatican's Belvedere.

1515. In Bologna, Leonardo is present at the meeting between Pope Leo X and King Francis I.

1516. Towards the end of the year, at the invitation of the King of France, he moves to the Château of Cloux, in Amboise.

1517. He is visited by Cardinal Louis of Aragon, to whom he shows his paintings and manuscripts.

1519, APRIL 23. He dictates his last will and testament.

1519, MAY 2. He dies at Cloux.

1519, AUGUST 12. Leonardo da Vinci is buried in the cloister of Saint Florentin in Amboise. During the Huguenot wars, in the second half of the sixteenth century, the church and tombs were generally ransacked, and his mortal remains were dispersed. Two centuries later some searches were begun by De Pagave, and later, in 1863, continued by A. Houssaye. All were unsuccessful.

DA VINCI'S PAINTINGS

Color Plate I

ANNUNCIATION, *Florence, Uffizi*, detail: The Virgin.

Plate 1

BAPTISM OF CHRIST. *Panel, 177 × 151.** Florence, Uffizi.* Painted about 1475 by Verrocchio and Leonardo. The latter was responsible for the angel seen in profile, holding the drapery, and for part of the landscape. The picture was first kept in the Cloister of San Salvi in Florence, then in Santa Verdiana. In 1810 it went to the Accademia di Belle Arti and in 1914 it was moved to the Uffizi. (See also plates 2 and 3.)

Plate 2

BAPTISM OF CHRIST, detail: background landscape, by Leonardo.

Plate 3

BAPTISM OF CHRIST, detail: The angels. The one on the left is by Leonardo.

Plate 4

THE BENOIS MADONNA. *Panel transferred on to canvas, 48 × 31. Leningrad, The Hermitage.* Painted about 1478. In the opinion of Adolfo Venturi this is one of the two Madonnas painted by Leonardo that year. In fact, the Master made a note of this on a sketch now in the Uffizi Gallery. Other preparatory sketches are in the British Museum, London.

Plate 5

MADONNA WITH VASE OF FLOWERS. *Panel, 62 × 47.* Munich, *Alte Pinakothek.* Painted about 1478-80. It may be the *Madonna with carafe*, described by Vasari as belonging to Pope Clement VII. This attribution is accepted by Bode, A. Venturi, and B. Berenson. (See also plates 6 and 7.)

Plate 6

MADONNA WITH VASE OF FLOWERS, detail: Landscape seen through the right-hand window.

Plate 7

MADONNA WITH VASE OF FLOWERS, detail: Head of the Virgin.

Plates 8-9

ANNUNCIATION. *Panel, 98 × 217. Florence, Uffizi.* Painted by Leonardo in Verrocchio's workshop about 1475-78. The picture was once kept in the Convent of San Bartolomeo di Monteoliveto, near Florence. Preparatory drawings are in Rome's Corsini Gallery, in the Louvre in Paris, and in Christ Church College, Oxford. The marble sarcophagus is a copy of that of Piero de' Medici executed by Verrocchio, in the Old Sacristy of San Lorenzo in Florence. The painting was hung in the Uffizi as a work attributed to Ghirlandaio. (See also plates 10-13 and color plate I.)

* All dimensions are given in centimetres.

Plate 10

ANNUNCIATION, detail: The Angel Gabriel.

Plate 11

ANNUNCIATION, detail: The Virgin's head and shoulders.

Plate 12

ANNUNCIATION, detail: Background landscape on the left.

Plate 13

ANNUNCIATION, detail: Background landscape in the center.

Plate 14

ANNUNCIATION. *Panel, 14 × 59. Paris, Louvre Museum.* Painted probably a short time before the previous one, this panel was the predella of the Madonna di Piazza painted by Lorenzo di Credi for the Pistoia Cathedral. The photograph shows the left side of the panel. (See also plate 15.)

Plate 15

ANNUNCIATION. Right side of panel.

Plate 16

PORTRAIT OF A WOMAN (*Ginevra de' Benci?*). *Panel, 42 × 37. Vaduz, Liechtenstein Gallery.* The plate shows the reverse of the panel (see color plate II), with the inscription: *"Virtutem forma decorat"* and a sprig of juniper encircled by a wreath of laurel and palm. The painting is in Leonardo's style.

Color Plate II

PORTRAIT OF A WOMAN (*Ginevra de' Benci?*). Painted about 1474-78. Some experts claim this to be the Ginevra de Benci portrait of which

Vasari wrote: "It is a wondrous thing." The attribution is not accepted by Morelli, Thiis, Cruttwell, Frizzoni, Siren, and Bodmer. (See also plates 16 and 17.)

Plate 17

PORTRAIT OF A WOMAN, detail of the face.

Plate 18

ADORATION OF THE MAGI. *Panel, 246 × 243, unfinished. Florence, Uffizi.* Painted about 1481-82 for the Convent of San Donato a Scopeto, near Florence. Fifteen years later the painting was replaced in the Convent by a similar subject by Filippo Lippi. Vasari saw Leonardo's panel in the home of Amerigo de' Benci. There are preparatory drawings for the general picture in the Uffizi, and others of its details in the Accademia, Venice, in the Louvre, in the Ecole des Beaux-Arts in Paris, in London's British Museum and in Oxford's Ashmolean Museum, in the Royal Library at Windsor Castle, in the Musée Bonnat at Bayonne, in Hamburg's Kunstalle, and in Cologne's Wallraf-Richartz Museum. (See also plates 19-23.)

Plate 19

ADORATION OF THE MAGI, detail: The central group.

Plate 20

ADORATION OF THE MAGI, detail: Architecture and horsemen in the left background.

Plate 21

ADORATION OF THE MAGI, detail: The adoring shepherds.

ntua. She asked him, instead, for 'young Christ, of about twelve rs".

Plate 57

CARTOON FOR ST ANNE, VIRGIN AND CHILD. *Charcoal on brown paper, 9 × 101. London, Burlington House (Royal Academy).* This was thought to have been commissioned for the main altar of the Church of Santissima Annunziata in Florence, and executed about 1501. If this were so, however, the picture would fit the description by Fra Pietro da Nuvolara, Isabella d'Este's secretary, on page 43. (See Selected Criticism.) The Burlington House cartoon, in the opinion of Sir Kenneth Clark, Eilwood McCurdy, and others, was executed in Milan before 1500. (See plates 58–61.)

Plate 58

CARTOON FOR ST ANNE, VIRGIN AND CHILD, detail: Head of the Virgin.

Plate 59

CARTOON FOR ST ANNE, VIRGIN AND CHILD, detail: Head of St Anne.

Plate 60

CARTOON FOR ST ANNE, VIRGIN AND CHILD, detail: The Child.

Plate 61

CARTOON FOR ST ANNE, VIRGIN AND CHILD, detail: St John.

Plate 62

MONA LISA. *Panel, 77 × 53. Paris, Louvre Museum.* Portrait of a young woman. On Vasari's authority the sitter was Monna Lisa Gherardini, wife of Francesco di Zanobi del Giocondo. Leonardo began this portrait in Florence in 1503, worked at the panel for four years, and even

then left it unfinished. The pa was among those taken by Master to France, where Francis I bought it for four thou golden ducats. In 1584 it was i Royal Collection at the Castl Fontainebleau. Its theft from Louvre on August 21, 1911, publicized all over the world. panel was recovered in Italy December 12, 1913. It was exhibi first in the Uffizi Gallery, then Rome's Borghese and Vatic Galleries, and later still in the Br Pinacoteca, Milan. Then it w returned to the Louvre. (See plat 63–65 and color plate IV.)

Plate 63

MONA LISA, detail: The head.

Plate 64

MONA LISA, detail: Background landscape on the left.

Color Plate IV

MONA LISA, details of face and background.

Plate 65

MONA LISA, detail: The hands.

Plate 66

ST ANNE, VIRGIN AND CHILD. *Panel, 168 × 112. Paris, Louvre Museum.* This is a development of the London cartoon (plate 57), executed about 1510. It is unfinished. Leonardo took it with him to France, where it was seen in Cloux by Antonio de Beatis, the secretary of Cardinal Louis of Aragon. The panel was brought back to Italy by the Master's pupil, Francesco Melzi, and in 1630 Cardinal Richelieu bought it in Casal Monferrato. From that date it became part of the French King's

Plate 22

ADORATION OF THE MAGI, detail: Horsemen in the left background.

Plate 23

ADORATION OF THE MAGI, detail: Battle-scene in the right background.

Plate 24

ST JEROME. *Panel, 103 × 75, unfinished. Rome, Pinacoteca Vaticana.* About 1482. Discovered in 1820 by Cardinal Flesch in a second-hand shop in Rome. (See also plate 25.)

Plate 25

ST JEROME, detail: Head of the Saint.

Plate 26

THE VIRGIN OF THE ROCKS. *Panel transferred to canvas, 198 × 123. Paris, Louvre Museum.* This is no longer believed to be the painting for which a contract was signed on April 25, 1483, between the Confraternity of the Immaculate Conception of St Francis in Milan and the artists Leonardo da Vinci, and Ambrogio and Evangelista De Predis. Nowadays it is certain that the original panel is in London (see next plate). The Louvre painting, therefore, would belong to Leonardo's early Florentine period, as Davies suggests, or at least to a period slightly before 1493. Preparatory drawings can be found in the Biblioteca Reale at Turin and in the Royal Library at Windsor Castle. (See also plates 28–33.)

Plate 27

THE VIRGIN OF THE ROCKS. *Panel, 189 × 119. London, National Gallery.* This was to be the central

panel of a large and elaborate altarpiece of many panels, some painted and some carved in wood. The painting was entrusted to Leonardo and the De Predis brothers by the Confraternity of the Immaculate Conception for their chapel in San Francesco Grande, in Milan. The commission was received in 1483. In 1508 the work was still unfinished. Most of the panel is not by Leonardo. (See also plates 34–39.)

Plate 28

THE VIRGIN OF THE ROCKS (*Louvre Museum*), detail: Head of the Virgin.

Plate 29

VIRGIN OF THE ROCKS, detail: Head of the Angel.

Plate 30

VIRGIN OF THE ROCKS, detail: St John.

Plate 31

VIRGIN OF THE ROCKS, detail: The Child Jesus.

Plate 32

VIRGIN OF THE ROCKS, detail: The rocks in the left background and the Virgin's head.

Plate 33

THE VIRGIN OF THE ROCKS, detail: The Angel: hands of the Virgin and the Angel.

Plate 34

THE VIRGIN OF THE ROCKS (*National Gallery*), detail: St John.

Plate 35

THE VIRGIN OF THE ROCKS, detail: Head of the Virgin.

Plate 36

THE VIRGIN OF THE ROCKS, detail: Rocks in the left background.

Plate 37

THE VIRGIN OF THE ROCKS, detail: Head of the Angel and the Virgin's hand.

Plate 38

THE VIRGIN OF THE ROCKS, detail: Bush in the right background, above the Angel's wing.

Plate 39

THE VIRGIN OF THE ROCKS, detail: Flowers in the left foreground.

Plates 40-41

THE LAST SUPPER. *Wall painting in oil tempera, 420 × 910. Milan, Refectory of the Convent of Santa Maria delle Grazie.* Painted between 1495 and 1497. It illustrates the episode of the Last Supper, related in the Four Gospels (Matthew xxvi, 17-29; Mark xiv, 12-25; Luke xxii, 7-23; John xiii, 21-30). This is the moment when Jesus announces that one of the Apostles will betray Him. Ludovico il Moro instructed Leonardo to paint the opposite wall of the Refectory as well, where Montorfano had already done a fresco of the Crucifixion, but in fact da Vinci only added the portraits of the Duke and Duchess with their children at the foot of the fresco (plates 54 and 55). In 1498 Pacioli wrote about *The Last Supper* as of a finished work. Preparatory drawings are kept in the Royal Library at Windsor Castle. Because of the unusual technique the painting deteriorated rapidly. In 1566 Vasari could only see "a muddle of blots". The painting has been restored many times. In 1943 the

refectory hall was badly bombed, but the wall on which *The Last Supper* was painted was practically undamaged. After a thorough reconstruction of the walls, in 1948, a final restoration of *The Last Supper* became possible. Mauro Pellicioli, having consolidated the original pigments, went on to clean the picture and methodically to remove the earlier restorations, so that in many places Leonardo's painting is now clearly visible. Pellicioli's work, completed in 1954, has been unanimously praised. Plates 46, 47, 48, and 49 show the picture after this last restoration. There are in existence many copies, some of which are extremely freely painted, of *The Last Supper*. A strictly documentary copy was painted by Giuseppe Bossi in 1807, but was later destroyed. (See also plates 42-49 and color plate III.)

Plate 42

THE LAST SUPPER, detail: The Apostles Bartholomew, James the Younger, and Andrew.

Plate 43

THE LAST SUPPER, detail: The Apostles, Judas, Peter and John.

Plate 44

THE LAST SUPPER, detail: The Apostles Thomas, James the Elder, and Philip.

Plate 45

THE LAST SUPPER, detail: The Apostles Matthew, Taddeus, and Simon.

Plate 46

THE LAST SUPPER, detail: Christ.

Plate 47

THE LAST SUPPER, detail: The Apostle Philip.

Plate 48

THE LAST SUPPER, detail: The hands of the Apostle Simon at the table.

Color Plate III

THE LAST SUPPER, detail: The Apostles in plate 43 and background.

Plate 49

THE LAST SUPPER, detail: The Apostles Thomas and James the Elder.

Plate 50

THE LAST SUPPER, detail: Lunette above the picture. In the three lunettes painted on the vault, Leonardo portrayed the Sforza coat of arms surrounded by garlands of fruit. This photograph shows one element in the garland painted in the central lunette. (See plates 51 and 52.)

Plate 51

THE LAST SUPPER, detail: Lunette above the picture. Detail of the garland in the lunette on the left.

Plate 52

THE LAST SUPPER, detail: Lunette above the picture. The complete lunette on the left, including the detail shown in the previous plate.

Plate 53

DECORATION OF THE VAULT OF THE SALA DELLE ASSE, IN THE CASTELLO SFORZESCO, MILAN. In a report by Gualtiero da Bascapè, written in 1498, Leonardo is said to have promised to finish this task "at

the end of Se
preparatory draw
found in the R
Windsor Castle,
Atlantico, and elsev
vault was freely rep
by Ernesto Rusca un
of Luca Beltrami. T
shows only one of
elements, which are al

Plate 54

PORTRAIT OF LU
MORO. *Milan Refectory
vent of Santa Maria delle
proximately 1498.* This
by Leonardo to the C
Donato da Montorfano,
process being superimpo
fresco. The chromatic pig
crumbled, and one can
perceive the outline of
profiles.

Plate 55

PORTRAIT OF BEATRICE L
LUDOVICO'S DUCHESS. Ac
Leonardo to Montorfano's
(See plate 54.)

Plate 56

CARTOON FOR A PORTRAIT
ISABELLA D'ESTE. *Silverpoint
and red chalk and touches of ye.
63 × 46. Paris, Louvre Museum.*
cartoon is mentioned in a let
written by Isabella to the art
Executed about 1499-1500. It w
bought by the Louvre in 1860 fro
the Vallardi Collection in Milar
Seidlitz, Hildebrandt, and Suida d
not accept the attribution. Isabella
herself, in a letter written on May
14, 1504, stated explicitly that she
no longer hoped that Leonardo
would keep his promise to color
the cartoon he had done of her in

Plate 22

ADORATION OF THE MAGI, detail: Horsemen in the left background.

Plate 23

ADORATION OF THE MAGI, detail: Battle-scene in the right background.

Plate 24

ST JEROME. *Panel, 103 × 75, unfinished. Rome, Pinacoteca Vaticana.* About 1482. Discovered in 1820 by Cardinal Flesch in a second-hand shop in Rome. (See also plate 25.)

Plate 25

ST JEROME, detail: Head of the Saint.

Plate 26

THE VIRGIN OF THE ROCKS. *Panel transferred to canvas, 198 × 123. Paris, Louvre Museum.* This is no longer believed to be the painting for which a contract was signed on April 25, 1483, between the Confraternity of the Immaculate Conception of St Francis in Milan and the artists Leonardo da Vinci, and Ambrogio and Evangelista De Predis. Nowadays it is certain that the original panel is in London (see next plate). The Louvre painting, therefore, would belong to Leonardo's early Florentine period, as Davies suggests, or at least to a period slightly before 1493. Preparatory drawings can be found in the Biblioteca Reale at Turin and in the Royal Library at Windsor Castle. (See also plates 28–33.)

Plate 27

THE VIRGIN OF THE ROCKS. *Panel, 189 × 119. London, National Gallery.* This was to be the central panel of a large and elaborate altarpiece of many panels, some painted and some carved in wood. The painting was entrusted to Leonardo and the De Predis brothers by the Confraternity of the Immaculate Conception for their chapel in San Francesco Grande, in Milan. The commission was received in 1483. In 1508 the work was still unfinished. Most of the panel is not by Leonardo. (See also plates 34–39.)

Plate 28

THE VIRGIN OF THE ROCKS (*Louvre Museum*), detail: Head of the Virgin.

Plate 29

VIRGIN OF THE ROCKS, detail: Head of the Angel.

Plate 30

VIRGIN OF THE ROCKS, detail: St John.

Plate 31

VIRGIN OF THE ROCKS, detail: The Child Jesus.

Plate 32

VIRGIN OF THE ROCKS, detail: The rocks in the left background and the Virgin's head.

Plate 33

THE VIRGIN OF THE ROCKS, detail: The Angel: hands of the Virgin and the Angel.

Plate 34

THE VIRGIN OF THE ROCKS (*National Gallery*), detail: St John.

Plate 35

THE VIRGIN OF THE ROCKS, detail: Head of the Virgin.

Plate 36

THE VIRGIN OF THE ROCKS, detail: Rocks in the left background.

Plate 37

THE VIRGIN OF THE ROCKS, detail: Head of the Angel and the Virgin's hand.

Plate 38

THE VIRGIN OF THE ROCKS, detail: Bush in the right background, above the Angel's wing.

Plate 39

THE VIRGIN OF THE ROCKS, detail: Flowers in the left foreground.

Plates 40–41

THE LAST SUPPER. *Wall painting in oil tempera, 420 × 910. Milan, Refectory of the Convent of Santa Maria delle Grazie.* Painted between 1495 and 1497. It illustrates the episode of the Last Supper, related in the Four Gospels (Matthew xxvi, 17–29; Mark xiv, 12–25; Luke xxii, 7–23; John xiii, 21–30). This is the moment when Jesus announces that one of the Apostles will betray Him. Ludovico il Moro instructed Leonardo to paint the opposite wall of the Refectory as well, where Montorfano had already done a fresco of the Crucifixion, but in fact da Vinci only added the portraits of the Duke and Duchess with their children at the foot of the fresco (plates 54 and 55). In 1498 Pacioli wrote about *The Last Supper* as of a finished work. Preparatory drawings are kept in the Royal Library at Windsor Castle. Because of the unusual technique the painting deteriorated rapidly. In 1566 Vasari could only see "a muddle of blots". The painting has been restored many times. In 1943 the refectory hall was badly bombed, but the wall on which *The Last Supper* was painted was practically undamaged. After a thorough reconstruction of the walls, in 1948, a final restoration of *The Last Supper* became possible. Mauro Pellicioli, having consolidated the original pigments, went on to clean the picture and methodically to remove the earlier restorations, so that in many places Leonardo's painting is now clearly visible. Pellicioli's work, completed in 1954, has been unanimously praised. Plates 46, 47, 48, and 49 show the picture after this last restoration. There are in existence many copies, some of which are extremely freely painted, of *The Last Supper*. A strictly documentary copy was painted by Giuseppe Bossi in 1807, but was later destroyed. (See also plates 42–49 and color plate III.)

Plate 42

THE LAST SUPPER, detail: The Apostles Bartholomew, James the Younger, and Andrew.

Plate 43

THE LAST SUPPER, detail: The Apostles, Judas, Peter and John.

Plate 44

THE LAST SUPPER, detail: The Apostles Thomas, James the Elder, and Philip.

Plate 45

THE LAST SUPPER, detail: The Apostles Matthew, Taddeus, and Simon.

Plate 46

THE LAST SUPPER, detail: Christ.

Plate 47

THE LAST SUPPER, detail: The Apostle Philip.

Plate 48

THE LAST SUPPER, detail: The hands of the Apostle Simon at the table.

Color Plate III

THE LAST SUPPER, detail: The Apostles in plate 43 and background.

Plate 49

THE LAST SUPPER, detail: The Apostles Thomas and James the Elder.

Plate 50

THE LAST SUPPER, detail: Lunette above the picture. In the three lunettes painted on the vault, Leonardo portrayed the Sforza coat of arms surrounded by garlands of fruit. This photograph shows one element in the garland painted in the central lunette. (See plates 51 and 52.)

Plate 51

THE LAST SUPPER, detail: Lunette above the picture. Detail of the garland in the lunette on the left.

Plate 52

THE LAST SUPPER, detail: Lunette above the picture. The complete lunette on the left, including the detail shown in the previous plate.

Plate 53

DECORATION OF THE VAULT OF THE SALA DELLE ASSE, IN THE CASTELLO SFORZESCO, MILAN. In a report by Gualtiero da Bascapè, written in 1498, Leonardo is said to have promised to finish this task "at the end of September". Partial preparatory drawings are to be found in the Royal Library at Windsor Castle, in the *Codice Atlantico*, and elsewhere. The entire vault was freely repainted in 1901–2 by Ernesto Rusca under the guidance of Luca Beltrami. The reproduction shows only one of the decorative elements, which are all similar.

Plate 54

PORTRAIT OF LUDOVICO IL MORO. *Milan Refectory of the Convent of Santa Maria delle Grazie.* Approximately 1498. This was added by Leonardo to the *Crucifixion* by Donato da Montorfano, the tempera process being superimposed on the fresco. The chromatic pigments have crumbled, and one can now only perceive the outline of the two profiles.

Plate 55

PORTRAIT OF BEATRICE D'ESTE, LUDOVICO'S DUCHESS. Added by Leonardo to Montorfano's fresco. (See plate 54.)

Plate 56

CARTOON FOR A PORTRAIT OF ISABELLA D'ESTE. *Silverpoint black and red chalk and touches of yellow, 63 × 46. Paris, Louvre Museum.* The cartoon is mentioned in a letter written by Isabella to the artist. Executed about 1499–1500. It was bought by the Louvre in 1860 from the Vallardi Collection in Milan. Seidlitz, Hildebrandt, and Suida do not accept the attribution. Isabella herself, in a letter written on May 14, 1504, stated explicitly that she no longer hoped that Leonardo would keep his promise to color the cartoon he had done of her in

Mantua. She asked him, instead, for a "young Christ, of about twelve years".

Plate 57

CARTOON FOR ST ANNE, VIRGIN AND CHILD. *Charcoal on brown paper, 139 × 101. London, Burlington House (Royal Academy).* This was thought to have been commissioned for the main altar of the Church of Santissima Annunziata in Florence, and executed about 1501. If this were so, however, the picture would fit the description by Fra Pietro da Nuvolara, Isabella d'Este's secretary, on page 43. (See Selected Criticism.) The Burlington House cartoon, in the opinion of Sir Kenneth Clark, Eilwood McCurdy, and others, was executed in Milan before 1500. (See plates 58–61.)

Plate 58

CARTOON FOR ST ANNE, VIRGIN AND CHILD, detail: Head of the Virgin.

Plate 59

CARTOON FOR ST ANNE, VIRGIN AND CHILD, detail: Head of St Anne.

Plate 60

CARTOON FOR ST ANNE, VIRGIN AND CHILD, detail: The Child.

Plate 61

CARTOON FOR ST ANNE, VIRGIN AND CHILD, detail: St John.

Plate 62

MONA LISA. *Panel, 77 × 53. Paris, Louvre Museum.* Portrait of a young woman. On Vasari's authority the sitter was Monna Lisa Gherardini, wife of Francesco di Zanobi del Giocondo. Leonardo began this portrait in Florence in 1503, worked at the panel for four years, and even then left it unfinished. The painting was among those taken by the Master to France, where King Francis I bought it for four thousand golden ducats. In 1584 it was in the Royal Collection at the Castle of Fontainebleau. Its theft from the Louvre on August 21, 1911, was publicized all over the world. The panel was recovered in Italy on December 12, 1913. It was exhibited first in the Uffizi Gallery, then in Rome's Borghese and Vatican Galleries, and later still in the Brera Pinacoteca, Milan. Then it was returned to the Louvre. (See plates 63–65 and color plate IV.)

Plate 63

MONA LISA, detail: The head.

Plate 64

MONA LISA, detail: Background landscape on the left.

Color Plate IV

MONA LISA, details of face and background.

Plate 65

MONA LISA, detail: The hands.

Plate 66

ST ANNE, VIRGIN AND CHILD. *Panel, 168 × 112. Paris, Louvre Museum.* This is a development of the London cartoon (plate 57), executed about 1510. It is unfinished. Leonardo took it with him to France, where it was seen in Cloux by Antonio de Beatis, the secretary of Cardinal Louis of Aragon. The panel was brought back to Italy by the Master's pupil, Francesco Melzi, and in 1630 Cardinal Richelieu bought it in Casal Monferrato. From that date it became part of the French King's collection. Many parts of the picture are the work of Leonardo's pupils. (See also plates 67–71.)

Plate 67

ST ANNE, VIRGIN AND CHILD, detail: The central group.

Plate 68

ST ANNE, VIRGIN AND CHILD, detail: Heads of St Anne and Virgin.

Plate 69

ST ANNE, VIRGIN AND CHILD, detail: The Child.

Plate 70

ST ANNE, VIRGIN AND CHILD, detail: Background on the left.

Plate 71

ST ANNE, VIRGIN AND CHILD, detail: Background on the right.

Plate 72

ST JOHN THE BAPTIST. *Panel, 69 × 57. Paris, Louvre Museum.* From a sketch in the *Codice Atlantico*, it would appear that this was painted during Leonardo's second period in Milan, between 1506 and 1513. Another preparatory sketch is in the Royal Library at Windsor Castle. The panel was seen at Cloux, in da Vinci's studio, in 1517. The French King Louis XIII gave it to Charles I, King of England, but in 1649 the French banker, Jabach, acquired it and made a present of it to Cardinal Mazarin, whose heirs sold it to King Louis XIV in 1661. It is considered Leonardo's last work. (See also plate 73.)

Plate 73

ST JOHN THE BAPTIST, detail: Face of the Saint.

Plate 74

MADONNA LITTA. This work is only traditionally attributed to Leonardo. (See Attributed Paintings.)

Plate 75

MADONNA LITTA, detail: The Virgin's head.

Plate 76

LADY WITH AN ERMINE. In the opinion of some critics this work is not by Leonardo. (See Attributed Paintings.) The ermine was frequently used as Duke Ludovico's emblem, and the sitter is thought to have been his mistress, Cecilia Gallerani.

Plate 77

LA BELLE FERRONIÈRE. Probably a work by Giovanni Antonio Boltraffio. (See Attributed Paintings and plate 81.)

Plate 78

PORTRAIT OF A MUSICIAN. The attribution is disputed. (See Attributed Paintings.) In the opinion of Sir Kenneth Clark this portrait, and the *Lady with an Ermine*, are by Leonardo's own hand.

Plate 79

PORTRAIT OF A LADY. (See Attributed Paintings.)

Plate 80

PORTRAIT OF A MUSICIAN, detail: The face.

Plate 81

LA BELLE FERRONIÈRE, detail: The face.

Plate 82

BACCHUS. (See Attributed Paintings.)

Plate 83

LEDA. (See Attributed Paintings and plate 84.)

Plate 84

STUDY FOR LEDA. An authentic drawing, now in the Royal Library at Windsor Castle.

Plate 85

HEAD OF A YOUNG WOMAN. Not proven to be a Leonardo original. (See Attributed Paintings.)

Plate 86

THE BATTLE OF ANGHIARI. (See Lost Paintings.) The photograph shows the oldest and most faithful copy of Leonardo's cartoon, by the hand of an anonymous artist, probably executed shortly after Leonardo's second journey to Milan in 1506. The sketch, which reproduces the central group of the picture, "The Struggle for the Standard", is kept in the Uffizi Gallery in Florence. (See also plates 87 and 88.)

Plate 87

THE BATTLE OF ANGHIARI. A second copy, by Rubens, of the picture's central group. It is kept in the Louvre in Paris.

Plate 88

THE BATTLE OF ANGHIARI. *Silverpoint and Sepia. Budapest, Museum of Fine Arts.* An authentic sketch by Leonardo for the heads of two warriors.

LOST PAINTINGS

TWO MADONNAS, painted by Leonardo in 1478 and mentioned by him on a sheet which is now in the Uffizi Gallery: " . . . ber 1478 I started to paint the two Marys". One of the two could be the one described in the *Anonimo Gaddiano* as "a panel of Our Lady, a most excellent thing". (See Bibliography.)

HEAD OF MEDUSA, recorded in the inventory of Duke Cosimo de' Medici's wardrobe.

ALTARPIECE for the Chapel of St Bernard in the Palazzo della Signoria, Florence (1478). The commission for this work had previously been given to Piero del Pollaiuolo. Leonardo's painting was not finished. On its pattern Filippo Lippi painted the *Madonna with Saints* now in the Uffizi.

PORTRAIT OF CECILIA GAL-LERANI (*circa* 1482). Praised by Bellincioni.

MADONNA, painted for the King of Hungary, Mathias Corvinus. Recorded in a letter from the Duke of Milan to his Ambassador, Maffeo Trevigliese (April 13, 1485).

PORTRAIT OF LUCREZIA CRI-VELLI (*circa* 1490). Leonardo recorded it in an epigram in his *Codice Atlantico*.

DECORATION OF THE "SALETTA NEGRA" in the Sforzesco Castle in Milan (1498). Documents illustrated by Muller-Walde.

MADONNA OF THE SPINDLES, painted in Florence (1501) for Florimond Robertet, Secretary of State to the King of France. Mentioned in a letter from Fra Pietro da Nuvolara to Isabella d'Este.

THE BATTLE OF ANGHIARI, painted for the Council Hall of the Palazzo Vecchio in Florence. In August, 1504 Leonardo and Michelangelo were asked by Gonfaloniere Piero Soderini to paint patriotic episodes on two walls of the Hall. Leonardo chose as his theme an incident from the war between the Florentines and the Milanese; Michelangelo chose a battle between Florence and Pisa. Da Vinci was allotted the Papal Hall in Santa Maria Novella to sketch his cartoon for the painting, which he finished in 1505, when he began to think about translating it into color. But there were many delays. By 1513 the painting was only completed in parts and protected by a special frame of wooden boards. Vasari wrote that Leonardo used here an unfortunate technical method, the Roman "encaustum", which caused the rapid decay and the ultimate obliteration of this work in 1557. Preparatory drawings are kept in the Venice Accademia, in London's British Museum, in the Royal Library at Windsor Castle, and in the Budapest Museum. Plate 86 shows a copy by an unknown artist of the central motif, the struggle for the Standard, which is kept in the Uffizi Gallery; another copy of the same group of horsemen, by P. P. Rubens, is in the Louvre (see plate 87). The original drawing by Leonardo for the heads of two warriors is now in the Budapest Museum (see plate 88).

A SECOND MEDUSA, given by Nicola Maffei to the Gonzaga family for the Royal Palace at Mantua (*circa* 1504). Recalled in a letter by Ippolito Calandra in 1531.

BACCHUS, owned in 1505 by Anton Maria Pallavicino, who was asked to sell it on behalf of the Duke of Ferrara. Commemorated in verse by Flavio Antonio Giraldi.

PETIT TABLEAU, a "Very excellent thing, received in January, 1507, by the King of France." Recorded by Gaye in *Unpublished documents of artists in the 14th, 15th and 16th centuries*. (Florence, 1840, II, 94.) The French King later insisted on more paintings from Leonardo, such as "certain small panels of Our Lady and somewhat else, depending on my fancy".

JUDITH, *circa* 1513, sent in 1569 from Rome to the Duke of Ferrara on behalf of Cardinal Ippolito II d'Este.

VIRGIN WITH CHILD AND BOY (1513–15), painted in Rome for Baldassarre Turini, a prelate of Pope Leo X. It was seen by Vasari in the Turini Collection in Pescia.

POMONA (*circa* 1515–19), executed for Francis I, King of France. Recalled by Lomazzo.

PAINTINGS ATTRIBUTED TO
DA VINCI

MADONNA LITTA. *Panel transferred to canvas, 42 × 33. Leningrad, the Hermitage.* This could be identified with the *Nursing Madonna*, seen in 1543 in the home of Michiel Contarini in Venice (from the *Anonimo Morelliano*), and later in the Litta house in Milan. In 1865 it was bought by Tzar Alexander II for the Hermitage Gallery, and was seriously damaged while being carried to Russia. A preparatory drawing of the Virgin's head is in the Louvre. It has also been attributed to Bernardino de Conti (by Morelli and Berenson), to Ambrogio De Predis (by Hildebrandt and Adolfo Venturi), and generally to Leonardo's school. The attribution to the Master is traditional. (See plate 75.)

LADY WITH AN ERMINE. *Panel, 54 × 39. Cracow, Czartoryski Museum.* Painted about 1490. The portrait has been alternately identified with Cecilia Gallerani and Beatrice d'Este. The attribution to Leonardo is accepted by Sir Kenneth Clark, Bode, Suida, Adolfo Venturi, and others. It is not accepted by Seidlitz, who ascribes it to Ambrogio De Predis, or by Gronau, Berenson, Siren, and Poggi, who see it as the work of Boltraffio. (See plate 76.)

LA BELLE FERRONIÈRE. *Panel, 62 × 44. Paris, Louvre Museum.* This is the traditional name given to the portrait of a young woman owing to a confusion in an early inventory.

Probably painted in the last decade of the fifteenth century. Though attributed to Leonardo, the painting is ascribed by some modern critics (Frizzoni, Seidlitz, Siren, Hildebrandt and others) to Boltraffio. Sir Kenneth Clark is "now inclined to think that the picture is by Leonardo". (*Leonardo da Vinci,* Pelican, revised edition.) (See plates 77 and 81.)

PORTRAIT OF A MUSICIAN (*Franchino Gaffuri?*). *Panel, 43 × 31. Milan, Pinacoteca Ambrosiana.* Painted in the last decade of the fifteenth century; unfinished. It was recorded under Leonardo's name in the Ambrosiana inventory in 1686. The attribution is held to be valid by Muller-Walde, Beltrami, Bode, Suida, and Sir Kenneth Clark. It is not accepted by Morelli, Seidlitz, Berenson, Adolfo Venturi, Hildebrandt, and others. Siren thinks it to be the work of Boltraffio. (See plates 78 and 80.)

PORTRAIT OF A LADY (*Beatrice d'Este?*). *Panel, 51 × 34. Milan, Pinacoteca Ambrosiana.* Painted during the last decade of the fifteenth century, it is included in the catalogue of Federico Borromeo's "Museum" (1618). The traditional attribution is accepted by Muller-Walde, Gronau, Beltrami, and Bode but not by Berenson, Hildebrandt, Siren, and Bodmer, who see in the picture the work of Ambrogio De Predis. Recently Roberto Longhi suggested the name of Lorenzo Costa. (See plate 79.)

BACCHUS. *Canvas, 177 × 115. Paris, Louvre Museum.* Painted about 1506. In 1626 it was seen in Fontainebleau Castle under the title, *St John in the Desert.* The attribution is traditional. Frizzoni and Seidlitz believe it to be the work of Cesare da Sesto, and the background to have been painted by Bernazzano.

LEDA. *Panel, 132 × 78. Rome, Spiridon Collection.* This is one of the many versions of the same theme, inspired by the Leda which Leonardo painted in Rome for Giuliano de Medici between 1513 and 1515. Preparatory drawings for the painting are kept in the Royal Library at Windsor Castle (see plate 84) and in the Boymans Museum in Rotterdam. Another version of the painting is to be found in the Borghese Gallery in Rome. The traditional attribution of the painting on plate 83 to Leonardo is accepted by Adolfo and Lionello Venturi, but the other critics reserve their judgement.

HEAD OF A YOUNG WOMAN. *Panel, 27 × 21. Parma, Pinacoteca.* Executed in the first decade of the fifteenth century, it is no more than a monochrome sketch. Similar sketches exist in the Van Horne Collection in Montreal and in the Johnson Collection in Philadelphia. The attribution is doubtful. Bottaro believes this work to be a study for the Leda. (See plate 85.)

LOCATION OF PAINTINGS

BUDAPEST

MUSEUM

Drawing for the Battle of Anghiari
(plate 88).

CRACOW

CZARTORYSKI MUSEUM

Lady with an Ermine (plate 76;
attribution).

FLORENCE

UFFIZI GALLERY

Baptism of Christ, by Andrea del
Verrocchio and Leonardo (plates
1, 2, 3).
Annunciation (plates 8–9, 10, 11,
12, 13, and color plate I).
Adoration of the Magi (plates 18, 19,
20, 21, 22, 23).

LENINGRAD

THE HERMITAGE

Madonna of the Flower, or the
Benois Madonna (plate 4).
Nursing Madonna, or *Madonna Litta*
(plates 74, 75; attribution).

LONDON

NATIONAL GALLERY

The Virgin of the Rocks (plates 27,
34, 35, 36, 37, 38, 39).

BURLINGTON HOUSE (ROYAL ACADEMY)

*Cartoon for St Anne, Virgin and
Child* (plates 57, 58, 59, 60, 61).

MILAN

REFECTORY OF SANTA MARIA DELLE GRAZIE

The Last Supper (plates 40–41, 42,
43, 44, 45, 46, 47, 48, 49, 50, 51,
52 and color plate III).
*Portrait of Ludovico il Moro and
Beatrice d'Este* (plates 54, 55).

CASTELLO SFORZESCO

*Decoration of the Vault of the Sala
delle Asse* (plate 53).

PINACOTECA AMBROSIANA

*Portrait of a musician (Franchino
Gaffuri?)* (plates 78, 80; attribution). *Portrait of a lady (Beatrice
d'Este?)* (plate 79; attribution).

MUNICH

ALTE PINAKOTHEK

Madonna with vase of flowers (plates
5, 6, 7).

PARIS

LOUVRE MUSEUM

Annunciation (plates 14, 15).
The Virgin of the Rocks (plates 26,
28, 29, 30, 31, 32, 33).
*Cartoon for a portrait of Isabella
d'Este* (plate 56).
Mona Lisa (plates 62, 63, 64, 65,
and color plate IV).
St Anne, Virgin and Child (plates
66, 67, 68, 69, 70, 71).
St John the Baptist (plates 72, 73).
La Belle Ferronière (plates 77, 81;
attribution).
Bacchus (plate 82; attribution).

41

PARMA

PINACOTECA

Head of a young woman (plate 85; attribution).

ROME

PINACOTECA VATICANA

St Jerome (plates 24, 25).

SPIRIDON COLLECTION

Leda (plate 83; attribution).

VADUZ

LIECHTENSTEIN GALLERY

Portrait of a woman (Ginevra de' Benci?) (plates 16, 17 and color plate II).

WINDSOR

ROYAL LIBRARY

Study for Leda (plate 84).

SELECTED CRITICISM

In the time of Ludovico Sforza, Viscount and Duke of Milan, some gentlemen were met one day in the monks' refectory of the convent delle Grazie, where with hushed voices they watched Leonardo da Vinci as he was finishing his marvellous picture of the *Last Supper*. The painter was well pleased that each should tell him what they thought of his work. He would often come to the convent at early dawn; and this I have seen him do myself. Hastily mounting the scaffolding, as the picture is somewhat high upon the ground, he worked on from dawn till sunset, until the shades of evening compelled him to cease, never thinking of food or drink. At other times he would remain two, three or four days without touching the painting, only coming for two or three hours to sit in front of it, considering and examining and judging his figures within himself.

At mid-day too, when the sun is in Leo, I have seen him hasten from the citadel, where he was modelling his stupendous horse in clay, and go directly to the convent, where he would mount the scaffolding, take up his brush, add a touch or two, then abruptly leave the place and go elsewhere.

MATTEO BANDELLO,
Novelle, 1497.

Leonardo's life is changeful and very uncertain; he gives the impression of living by the day. Since he has been in Florence he has worked just on one cartoon, which represent an infant Christ of about one year, freeing himself almost out of his mother's arms, and seizing a lamb and apparently about to embrace it. The mother, half rising from St Anne's lap, is taking the Child to draw it from the lamb, that sacrificial animal, which signifies the Passion. While St Anne, rising slowly from her seat, seems as if she would hold back her daughter, so that she would not separate the Child from the lamb, which perhaps signifies that the Church did not wish to prevent the Passion of Christ. These figures are life-size, but they are in a small cartoon because all are seated or bent, and each one is placed before the other, to the left. The sketch is not yet complete.

P. DA NUVOLARA,
Letter to Isabella d'Este, 1497.

Yet another of the greatest artists in the world scorns the art in which so very few can equal him, and has begun to study philosophy, about which he has such strange and fanciful new notions and concepts that, for all his writings, he is not able to portray it.

B. CASTIGLIONE,
Il Cortegiano, 1508.

Léonard de Vinci, miroir profond et sombre,
Où des anges charmants, avec un doux sourire
Tout chargé de mystère, apparaissent a l'ombre
Des glaciers et des pins qui forment leur pays.

C. BAUDELAIRE,
Les fleurs du mal, 1857.

Nature had favored him so much that, wherever he turned his thoughts, his brains and his spirit, he showed such divinity that no one else could equal the perfection of his readiness, vivacity, goodness, imagination and beauty. One finds that Leonardo had such an understanding of art that, though he began many things, he finished none, because it seemed to him that his hand could add nothing to the artistic perfection of the things he had imagined. His mind conceived works so difficult that his hands, excellent though they were, could never have expressed them. His interests were so numerous that his inquiries into natural phenomena led him to study the properties of herbs and to

44

observe the movements of the heavens, the moon's orbit and the progress of the sun.

GIORGIO VASARI,
Le vite, 1568.

In giving lights to his pictures Leonardo seems to have been constantly afraid of adding too much luminosity, as if he chose to save the lights for a better moment; he therefore sought the deepest blacks in order to render the lights clearer by contrast. Thanks to this method he reproduced, in his wonderful faces and figures, all that nature itself can do. And in this he was superior to all, so that one may safely claim that Leonardo's lights were divine.

G. P. LOMAZZO,
The Idea of the Temple of Painting, 1590.

Leonardo da Vinci began by examining each object in the light of an exact theory, and then proceeded to explain it against the natural background that he wanted to use. He respected conventions and abstained from all affectation. He knew how to impart to each thing the liveliest, the most specific and convenient character, and could enhance the concept of majesty to the point of making it divine. The rule that he followed in his expressions was to fire people's imagination by attracting it with essentials rather than confusing it with trivialities, and in this he strove to be neither prodigal nor avaricious.

P. P. RUBENS,
in R. de Piles: *Summary of the life of painters*, 1699.

The many gifts bestowed upon him by nature were embodied mainly in his eyes; though he was a universal genius, Leonardo was first and foremost a great painter. Regularly and perfectly formed, he appeared, next to common humanity, as an ideal specimen of it. Just as clarity and perception of sight are generally referred to the intelligence, so clarity and intelligence were typical of him. He never surrendered to the extreme impulses of

45

his original and unequalled talent and, by controlling each spontaneous and casual transport, ensured that every line he drew was the product of thorough meditation. From his studies of pure proportions to the extraordinary and contradictory figures of his most hybrid monsters, everything had to appear natural and rational.

W. GOETHE,
Art and antiquity, 1817.

He had that rare nobility of drawing in greater measure than Raphael, because he did not blend the expression of force with nobility. His coloring was sad and tender, rich with shadows, devoid of splendor even in the most brilliant colors, so that it triumphed in the chiaroscuro. If it had not existed it should have been invented for such a picture. (*The Last Supper.*)

STENDHAL,
History of Italian painting, 1817.

As an artist, Leonardo possesses all the most contradictory characteristics. While incessantly engaged in discovering, through anatomy, the causes of each corporeal form and of its movements, he applies the same sudden and assured intuition to spiritual expressions, and seeks them all, from heavenly beauty to depravity and buffoonery. This is best proven by his pen and ink sketches. In him the purest lyricism is combined to the profoundest strength of thought and to the highest awareness of the principles governing ideal compositions. He is more realistic than his predecessors wherever realism is possible, and furthermore he conveys a feeling of serenity and freedom as few others can do in any century.

J. BURCKHARDT,
The Cicerone, 1855.

From childhood we see this image (the *Mona Lisa*) defining itself on the fabric of his dreams; and but for express historical testimony we might fancy that this was but his ideal lady, embodied and beheld at last. What was the relationship of a living Florentine to this creature of his thought? By what strange affinities had the dream and the person grown up thus apart, and yet so closely together? Present from the first incorporeally in Leonardo's brain, dimly traced in the designs of Verrocchio, she is found present at last in *Il Giocondo's* house. That there is much of mere portraiture in the picture is attested by the legend that by artificial means, the presence of mimes and flute-players, that subtle expression was protracted on the face. Again, was it in four years and by renewed labor never really completed, or in four months and as by stroke of magic that the image was projected?

. . . The presence that rose so strangely beside the waters is expressive of what in the ways of a thousand years men had come to desire. Hers is the head upon which all "the ends of the world are come", and the eyelids are a little weary. It is beauty wrought out from within the flesh, the deposit, little cell by cell, of strange thoughts and fantastic reveries and exquisite passions. Set it for a moment beside one of those white Greek goddesses of beautiful women of antiquity, and how would they be troubled by this beauty, into which the soul with all its maladies has passed! All the thoughts and experience of the world have etched and moulded there, in that which they have of power to refine and make expressive the outward form, the animalism of Greece, the lust of Rome, the mysticism of the middle age with its spiritual ambition and imaginative loves, the return of the Pagan world, the sins of the Borgias.

. . . She is older than the rocks among which she sits; like the vampire, she has been dead many times and learnt the secrets of the grave; and has been a diver in deep seas, and keeps their fallen day about her; and trafficked for strange webs with Eastern merchants; and, as Leda, was the mother of Helen of Troy, and, as St Anne, the mother of Mary; and all this has been to her but as the sound of lyres and flutes, and lives only in the delicacy with which it has moulded the changing lineaments, and tinged the eyelids and the hands. The fancy of a perpetual life, sweeping together ten thousand experiences, is an old one; and modern philosophy has conceived the idea of humanity as wrought upon by, and summing up in himself, all modes of thought and life. Certainly Lady Lisa might stand as the embodiment of the old fancy, the symbol of the modern idea.

W. PATER,
The Renaissance, 1873.

Leonardo is *par excellence* the painter of mystery, of the ineffable, of dusk; his pictures appear as music in a minor key. His shadows are veils through which he leaves an opening, or which he thickens, to let us guess at a secret thought. His tones fade out as colors do in the moonlight, his contours roll away and are drowned, as if blown out by a sinister breeze, and the passage of time, harmful to other artists, is advantageous to him, because it deepens those harmonious shadows into which he loves to submerge himself.

T. GAUTIER,
Italian journey, 1875.

I know of nothing greater against this genius than scientific pharisaism. If he analyses what nature has achieved, he does it in order to compete with nature; if he thinks, it is because he intends to act. He is contemptuous of fanciful notions, but entirely dedicated to his ideal; above all he loves invention.

... To speak the truth, Da Vinci's realism is the most wonderful faith of the spirit. ... One should not expect of him the charm of simple souls. He is not one of those who can lose themselves in others, not the oak-tree that leans upon the ivy. He gives himself to those who really deserve it; he never betrays the natural object of his love and without ever refusing himself to his fellows, he follows his natural inclination towards what is eternal and divine.

G. DE SEAILLES,
Leonardo da Vinci, artist and scientist, 1892.

How strange! This most methodical of men, who among the masters of his time was the most occupied with methods of execution, and taught them with such thoroughness that the works of his best pupils are still confused with his own, this man whose "manner" was so characteristic—he was devoid of all "rhetoric". Always watchful of nature, which he consulted incessantly, he yet never imitated himself. This most erudite of masters was also the most ingenuous, and neither of his two emulators, Michelangelo or Raphael, deserved this praise.

E. DELACROIX,
Diary, 1893.

All that Giotto and Masaccio had attained in the rendering of tactile values, all that Fra Angelico or Filippo had achieved in expression, all that Pollaiuolo had accomplished in movement, or Verrocchio in light and shade, Leonardo, without the faintest trace of that tentativeness, that painfulness of effort which characterized his immediate precursors, equalled or surpassed. Outside Velazquez, and perhaps, when at their best, Rembrandt and Degas, we shall seek in vain for tactile values so stimulating and so convincing as those of his "Mona Lisa"; outside Degas, we shall not find much supreme mastery over the art of movement as in the unfinished "Epiphany" in the Uffizi; and if Leonardo has been left far behind as a painter of light, no one has succeeded in conveying by means of light and shade a more penetrating feeling of mystery and awe than he in his "Virgin of the Rocks". Add to all this a feeling for beauty and significance that have scarcely ever been approached. . . . Leonardo is the one artist of whom it may be said with perfect literalness: Nothing that he touched but turned into a thing of eternal beauty. Whether it be the cross-section of a skull, the structure of a weed, or a study of muscles, he, with his feeling for line and for light and shade, for ever transmuted it into life-communicating values; all without intention, for most of these magical sketches were dashed off to illustrate purely scientific matter, which alone absorbed his mind at the moment.

49

. . . Painting, then, was to Leonardo so little of a pre-occupation that we must regard it as merely a mode of expression used at moments by a man of universal genius, who recurred to it only when he had no more absorbing occupation, and only when it could express what nothing else could, the highest spiritual through the highest material significance. . . . We are too apt to regard a universal genius as a number of ordinary brains somehow conjoined in one skull, and not always on the most neighborly terms. We forget that genius means mental energy, and that a Leonardo, for the self-same reason that prevents his being merely a painter—the fact that it does not exhaust a hundredth part of his energy—will, when he does turn to painting, bring to bear a power of seeing, feeling and rendering, as utterly above that of the ordinary painter as the "Mona Lisa" is above, let us say, Andrea del Sarto's "Portrait of his Wife". No, let us not join in the reproaches made to Leonardo for having painted so little; because he had much more to do than to paint, he has left all of us heirs to one or two of the supremest works of art ever created.

B. BERENSON,
The Italian Painters of the Renaissance, 1896.

Perhaps the world knows of no other example of a genius so universal, so endowed with imagination, so unsatisfiable, so thirsting for the eternal, so naturally subtle, so pushed forward beyond his own century and the centuries to come. His figures express incredible spirit and sensitivity; they are spilling over with ideas and unexpressed feeling.

H. TAINE,
Italian Journey, 1897.

One will immediately notice how the composition of the panel (*St Anne, Virgin and Child*) can be geometrically inscribed into an isosceles triangle. This is the result of a search already discernible in the *Virgin of the Rocks*. Leonardo tried to coordinate his composition into a simple geometrical form.

rom the first he is obsessed by vital force and finds it expressed
plants and creatures; then, as his scientific researches develop
e learns the vast power of natural forces and he pursues science
s a means by which these forces can be harnessed for human
advantage. The further he penetrates the more he becomes
aware of man's impotence; his studies of hydrodynamics suggest
a power of water beyond human control; his studies of geology
show that the earth has undergone cataclysmic upheavals of
which ordinary earthquakes are but faint and distant echoes; his
studies of embryology point to a central problem of creation
apparently insoluble by science. The intellect is no longer supreme,
and human beings cease to be the center of nature; so they
gradually fade from his imagination, or when they appear, as St
Anne or St John, they are human no longer but symbols of
force and mystery, messengers from a world which Leonardo da
Vinci, the disciple of experience, has not explored, though he has
earned the right to proclaim its existence. *La natura è piena
d'infinite ragioni che non furomo mai in esperienza.*

KENNETH CLARK,
Leonardo da Vinci, 1939.

By softening his outlines, and by attracting the edges of his
objects towards a faraway point which was no longer the
abstract focus of forward perspective, but was a remote undulat-
ing focus, much diluted with blues, Leonardo created a space
which had never been seen in Europe, a space which was no
longer just the container of bodies, but attracted characters and
spectators as well in their relation to time. This "sfumato" was
necessary so that Titian could, one day, break out of the outline,
so that Rembrandt, the sorcerer, might one day be born.

A. MALRAUX,
Psychology of art, 1950.

Having left the Florence of line and of plastic shape, he dreamt
of a new pictorial world immersed in the mystery of shadow, as
changeable as atmosphere and light. . . .

. . . Leonardo's attempt to constrict into an ever smaller space
an ever growing intensity of movement was not an artifice: his
power of expression increased accordingly.

H. WOELFFLIN,
Classic Art, 1899.

This exceptional artist is better understood by his thoughts than
by his eyes. The needs of a Leonardo da Vinci are appeased in the
realm of thought, there being no necessity for voluptuous
realization. His intelligence could have rebelled, never his nerves.
The contemporaries of this great genius understood him.
Lomazzo called him a Hermes, a Prometheus, and he appeared to
them all as a sorcerer who knew the secret of all things. He knew
the laws of life. This is evident from his masterpiece. How the
figure of Jesus, which is the center of *The Last Supper*, was going
to be studied and elaborated by him! The truth is that, for some,
the figure represents also the center of our human conscience.

M. BARRÈS,
A visit to Leonardo da Vinci, 1908.

No artist was readier to assimilate the forms of expression
inherited from the past, and to create new ones; no one better
than he was able to control form and to become the living vehicle
of his own artistic idea. One can recognize a further aspect of
Florentine energy in the gusto with which Leonardo spotted the
salient points and the characteristic traits of everything. The
fundamental note, so to speak, of his art, is essentially Florentine,
but he was able to discover harmonies of a richness totally unknown, before him, to his country's art.

O. SIREN,
Leonardo da Vinci, 1911.

Leonardo begins from inside, from mental space, not from the
lines of a well defined contour, and finishes—when he does—by
spreading the substance of color as a breeze might do, aiming at
the conception of the corporeal image itself. This is absolutely
indescribable. Raphael's paintings are laid down in "planes", in

which the various harmonical groups are divided, and a background encloses the ensemble with a great sense of measure. Leonardo knows only space, vast, eternal, in which the figures are seen, as it were, to glide. The former offers, in the frame of his image, a sum of objects separate and contiguous; the latter offers a portion of the Infinite.

O. SPENGLER,
Decline of the West, 1917.

This symbolic spirit is the possessor of the greatest assortment of forms, of an ever perspicuous treasure of suggestions inspired to him by nature, of a constantly urging vigor which increases with the expansion of his domain. He is substantiated by a multitude of beings, of memories, and by his capacity for recognizing, in the immensity of the world, an extraordinary number of separate things and for arranging them in a thousand different ways. He is a master of faces, of anatomies, of machines. He knows what makes up a smile, and can impress it on the front of a house, or in the nooks of a garden; he can smooth out or disturb the waters of a brook and the tongues of a flame. If his hand is giving shape to the episodes of the battles he has imagined, then the trajectories of a thousand projectiles exploding upon the city's defences and upon the squares—created and fortified by him—become formidable floreal blooms. As one who thinks that in peace time things change too slowly, he dreams of battles, of storms, of torrential rain. He is accustomed to seeing them in all their mechanical complexity and to distinguish the apparent independence or the fragmentary existence of a handful of sand tossed in the wind, or the dispersed idea of each warrior moved by a passion or by an intimate sorrow.

P. VALÉRY,
Introduction to the method of Leonardo da Vinci, 1919.

What Leonardo suggests when he draws, he translates into action when he paints: air, light, movement. This is what for centuries has been demanded of color, and Leonardo has no color. He found in Florence a color that was lively, and apt to add

preciousness to a solid surface. He rejected it, be[...] interested in solid surfaces. His eye was too take[...] horizons of the flat valleys, broken here and the[...] and enclosed by the mountains. What could a solid[...] against the sight of those wide distant skylines? Ye[...] suited to define a human body seen at short d[...] Leonardo's eye wanted to see at a distance the hum[...] well. Everything, if too close, appears to be still,[...] eternal oscillation of the atmosphere makes every dist[...] seem light, almost hovering in the air. And the eveni[...] when dusk envelops souls and objects, imparts to the [...] slow, uninterrupted vibration. Dusk, atmosphere, physic[...] ment of each molecule of the Universe, spiritual vibrati[...] in a dream, the faraway vagueness of compenetrating mas[...] these things he brought into the human figure. Shape w[...] shape, color without color. A chromatic vision of fo[...] formal realization of color. . . . Matter is color when it i[...] transformed into an effect of light; matter is but a sha[...] marble. And Leonardo's eye, forever observing the spirit[...] things, rejected all matter. As he exalted the eye, he scorned [...] supreme pleasures of the eye, such as a beautifully levigate[...] marble, or a dazzling precious stone. He always went furthe[...] breathlessly searching for the quality of things, and therefor[...] rejecting things. Splendid colors and solid forms were too easy for him. What synthesis could one draw from them? What glance could be so high as to embrace the whole Universe in its unity, free from all details of circumstance? None. One, therefore, could only strive continuously, noting the continuity of passage, of movement. But when one puts color on to canvas, how can he express the yearnings of the soul and the movement of things? Where is a visible fluid which is neither color nor form but includes them both? This fluid is Leonardo's art. It represents his spirit in its constant labor, made up of love and intelligence.

L. VENTURI,
The criticism and art of Leonardo da Vinci, 1919.

In the Renaissance, which unified human activities art meant science, art meant truth of truth; in this Da Vinci acquired his significance and his greatness, that he took upon himself the epic of Italian art to conquer what was universal: this man, who combined in himself the artist's fluctuating sensitivity and the deep-rooted logic of the scientist. This man, who was poet and master.

A. VENTURI,
"Leonardo da Vinci's art" in *Enciclopedia Italiana*, 1954.

BIBLIOGRAPHICAL NOTE

The reader is referred to the most reliable ancient sources, such as the *Anonimo Gaddiano* (years from 1506 to 1532, *Codice Magliabecchiano XVII*, 17, of the Biblioteca Nazionale in Florence), Vasari's *Lives* (1st edition, Florence 1550), the *Trattato* and *The Idea of the Temple of Painting* by G. P. Lomazzo (Milan 1548 and Milan 1590). Two fundamental works should be noted: E. Verga, *Bibliografia Vinciana*, Bologna 1931; and L. Beltrami, *Documenti e memorie riguardanti la vita e le opere di Leonardo da Vinci*, Milan 1919.

The following may also be consulted:

L. PACIOLI. *Divina Proportione*, Venice 1509.

CARLO AMORETTI. *Memorie storiche sulla viat . . . de Leonardo da Vinci*, Milan 1804.

G. BOSSI. *Del Cenacolo di Leonardo da Vinci*, Milan 1810.

W. PATER. *The Renaissance, Studies in art and poetry*, London 1873.

J. P. RICHTER. *The literary works of Leonardo da Vinci*, London 1883.

P. UZIELLI. *Ricerche intorno a Leonardo da Vinci*, Rome 1884.

P. MULLER-WALDE. *Léonardo da Vinci: Lebensskisse und Forschungen über sein Verhältnis zur florent. Kunst und zu Rafael*, Munich 1889–90.

ANONIMO. *In Codice Magliabecchiano*, ed. Carl Frey, Berlin 1892.

G. DE SÉAILLES. *Léonard de Vinci, l'artiste et le savant*, Paris 1892.

E. MÜNTZ. *Léonard de Vinci: l'artiste, le penseur, le savant*, Paris 1899.

EDMONDO SOLMI. *Leonardo*, Florence 1900.

A. L. WOLINSKY. *Leonardo da Vinci*, St Petersburg 1900.

H. HORNE (trans.). *The Life of Leonardo da Vinci* by Giorgio Vasari, London 1903.

E. MCCURDY. *Leonardo da Vinci*, London 1904.

L. BELTRAMI. *Il Cenacolo di Leonardo da Vinci*, Milan 1908.

W. VON SEIDLITZ. *Leonardo da Vinci, der Wendepunkt der Renaissance*, Berlin 1909.

J. THIIS. *Leonardo da Vinci*, Oslo 1909.

SIGMUND FREUD. *Eine Kindheitserinnerung des Leonardo da Vinci*, Vienna 1910.

O. SIREN. *Leonardo da Vinci*, Stockholm 1911.

A. J. ANDERSEN. *The admirable painter. A study on Leonardo da Vinci*. London 1915.

F. MALAGUZZI VALERI. *La Corte di Ludovico il Moro*. Milan 1915 (2 vols.).

B. BERENSON. *The study and criticism of Italian art*, London 1916 (3 vols.).

PAUL VALERY. *Introduction à la méthode de Léonard de Vinci*, Paris 1919.

L. VENTURI. *La critica e l'arte di Leonardo da Vinci*, Bologna 1919.

G. POGGI. *Leonardo da Vinci. La vita di Giorgio Vasari commentata nuovamente ed illustrata*, Florence 1919.

A. VENTURI. *Leonardo da Vinci pittore*, Bologna 1920.

W. VON BODE. *Studien über Leonardo da Vinci*, Berlin 1921.

G. B. DE TONI. *Le piante e gli animali in Leonardo da Vinci*, Bologna 1922.

E. SOLMI. *Scritti pinciani*, Florence 1924.

G. CALVI. *I manoscritti di Leonardo da Vinci*, Bologna 1925.

A. DE RINALDIS. *Storia dell'opera pittorica di Leonardo da Vinci*, Bologna 1926.

E. HILDEBRANDT. *Leonardo da Vinci*, Berlin 1927.

A. R. TAYLOR. *Leonardo the Florentine. A study in personality*, London 1927.

A. OBERDORFER. *Leonardo da Vinci*, Turin 1928.

A. E. POPP. *Leonardo da Vinci Zeichnungen*, Munich 1928.

E. MCCURDY. *The mind of Leonardo da Vinci*, London 1928.

W. SUIDA. *Leonardo und sein Kreis*, Munich 1929.

BIBLIOGRAPHIA. ETTORE VERGA. *Bibliographia Vinciana 1493–1930*, Bologna 1931.

H. BODMER. *Leonardo*, Stoccarda-Berlin 1931.

R. MAZZUCCONI. *Leonardo da Vinci*, Florence 1932.

G. DE LA TOURETTE. *Léonard de Vinci*, Paris 1932.

E. MCCURDY. *Leonardo da Vinci, the artist*, London 1933.

K. CLARK. *A catalogue of the drawings of Leonardo da Vinci in the collection of His Majesty the King at Windsor Castle*, Cambridge 1935.

G. CALVI. *Vita di Leonardo*, Brescia 1936.

F. BÉRENCE. *Léonard de Vinci, ouvrier de l'intelligence*, Paris 1938.

E. MCCURDY. *Leonardo da Vinci's notebooks*, Florence 1938.

C. WEISMANTEL. *Leonardo da Vinci*, Cologne 1938.

K. CLARK. *Leonardo da Vinci: an account of his development as an Artist*, Cambridge 1939; second edition 1952.

G. NICODEMI. *Leonardo da Vinci*, Zurich 1939.

A. VENTURI. *Leonardo e la sua scuola*, Novara 1941.

H. LEPORINI. *Handzeichnungen grosser Meister, Leonardo da Vinci*, Berlin 1941.

S. BOTTARI. *Leonardo*, Bergamo 1942.

L. H. HEYDENREICH. *Leonardo*, Berlin 1943; second edition London-Basilea 1954.

L. GOLDSCHEIDER. *Leonardo da Vinci*, London-New York 1943.

D. R. LANGTON. *Leonardo da Vinci. His life and his pictures*, Chicago 1944.

A. E. POPHAM. *The drawings of Leonardo da Vinci*, London 1946.

M. DAVIES. *Leonardo da Vinci. The Virgin of the Rocks in the National Gallery*, London 1947.

G. ROCCO. *Quel che e avvenuto al Cenacolo Vinciano*, Milan 1947.

H. DUMONT. *Léonard de Vinci*, Paris 1949.

L. H. HEYDENREICH. *I disegni di Leonardo da Vinci e della sua scuola conservati nella Galleria dell'Accademia di Venezia*, Florence 1949.

A. MALRAUX. *Tout l'œuvre peint de Léonard de Vinci*, Montrouge 1950.

A. VALLENTIN. *Léonard de Vinci*, 2nd edition, Paris 1950.

H. BEENKEN. "Madonna in Felsengrotte", in *Festschrift für H. Jantzen*, Berlin 1951.

F. FLORA. *Leonardo*, Milan 1952.

G. CASTELFRANCO. "Introduzione a Leonardo", in *Nuova Antologia*, Rome 1952.

L. GOLDSCHEIDER. *Leonardo da Vinci: Landscapes and plants*, London 1952.

L. VENTURI. "Pensiero e fantasia nell'arte di Leonardo da Vinci", in *Atti dell'Accademia Nazionale dei Lincei*, Rend. VII, 1952.

P. D'ANCONA. *Leonardo da Vinci*, Milan 1952.

Leonardo, Saggi e ricerche, Rome, Libreria dello Stato 1954.

MARCEL BRION. *Leonardo da Vinci*, London 1955.

REPRODUCTIONS

ACKNOWLEDGEMENT FOR
REPRODUCTIONS

Plates 1, 3, and 40–41, *Anderson*; plates 2, 12, 44, and 80, *Brogi*; plate 4, *The Hermitage, Leningrad*; plates 10, 11, 13, 20 to 23, 25, 26, 28 to 33, 42, 43, 45, 56, 57, 60 to 62, 78, 79, 85, and 87, *Alinari*; plates 27 and 34 to 39, *National Gallery, London*; plates 46, 47, 48, and 49, *Laboratorio Ricerche Scientifiche della Pinacoteca di Brera*. The photographs for all other plates in black and white have been kindly lent by the da Vinci Collection of the Castello Sforzesco in Milan.

Color plates: I, *Sovrintendenza alle Gallerie di Firenze*; II, *Conzett & Huber, Zurich*; III, *Claudio Emmer, Milan*; IV, photographic archives of Rizzoli Editore, Milan.

ANNUNCIATION, Florence, Uffizi. (*Detail of plates 8–9*)

Plate 1. Verrocchio and Leonardo: BAPTISM OF CHRIST, Florence,
Uffizi

Plate 2. *Detail of plate 1*

Plate 3. *Detail of plate 1*

Plate 4. MADONNA OF THE FLOWER (BENOIS MADONNA),
Leningrad, The Hermitage

Plate 5. MADONNA WITH VASE OF FLOWERS, Munich, Alte
Pinakothek

Plate 6. *Detail of plate 5*

Plate 7. *Detail of plate 5*

Plates 8–9. ANNUNCIATION, Florence, Uffizi

Plate 10. *Detail of plates 8–9*

Plate 11. *Detail of plates 8–9*

Plate 12. *Detail of plates 8–9*

Plate 13. *Detail of plates 8–9*

Plate 14. ANNUNCIATION, Paris, Louvre (left panel)

Plate 15. ANNUNCIATION, Paris, Louvre (right panel)

Plate 16. Reverse of *Ginevra de' Benci*

PORTRAIT OF A WOMAN (GINEVRA DE' BENCI ?),
Vaduz, Liechtenstein Gallery

Plate 17. *Detail of color plate II*

Plate 18. ADORATION OF THE MAGI, Florence, Uffizi

Plate 19. *Detail of plate 18*

Plate 20. *Detail of plate 18*

Plate 21. *Detail of plate 18*

Plate 22. *Detail of plate 18*

Plate 23. *Detail of plate 18*

Plate 24. ST JEROME, Rome, Vatican Gallery

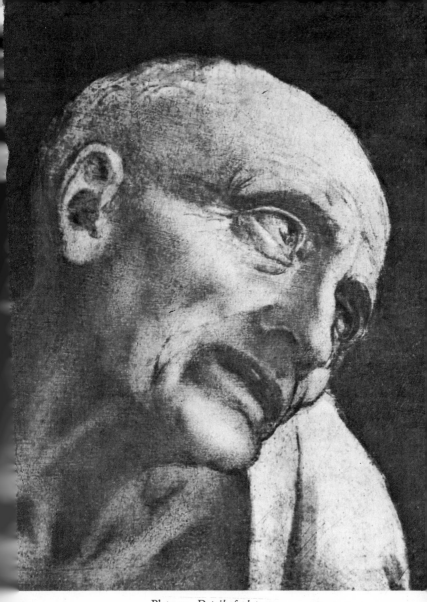

Plate 25. *Detail of plate 24*

Plate 26. THE VIRGIN OF THE ROCKS, Paris, Louvre

Plate 27. THE VIRGIN OF THE ROCKS, London, National Gallery

Plate 28. *Detail of plate 26*

Plate 29. *Detail of plate 26*

Plate 30. *Detail of plate 26*

Plate 31. *Detail of plate 26*

Plate 32. *Detail of plate 26*

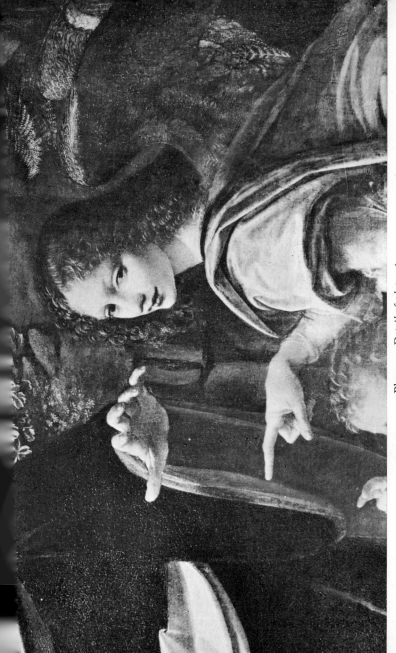

Plate 33. *Detail of plate 26*

Plate 34. *Detail of plate 27*

Plate 35. *Detail of plate 27*

Plate 36. *Detail of plate 27*

Plate 37. *Detail of plate 27*

Plate 38. *Detail of plate 27*

Plate 39. *Detail of plate 27*

Plates 40–41. THE LAST SUPPER, Milan, Refectory of Santa Maria
delle Grazie

Plate 42. *Detail of plates 40–41*

Plate 43. *Detail of plates 40–41*

Plate 44. *Detail of plates 40–41*

Plate 45. *Detail of plates 40–41*

Plate 46. *Detail of plates 40–41*

Plate 47. *Detail of plates 40–41*

Plate 48. *Detail of plates 40–41*

THE LAST SUPPER, Milan, Santa Maria delle Grazie. (*Detail of plates 40–41*)

Plate 49. *Detail of plates 40–41*

Plate 50. Central lunette above *The Last Supper* (*detail*)

Plate 51. *Detail of plate 52*

Plate 52. Lunette above left of *The Last Supper*

Plate 53. Vault of the Sala delle Asse, Milan, Castello Sforzesco (*detail*)

Plate 54. Ludovico il Moro, in the *Crucifixion* by Montorfano, Milan,
Santa Maria delle Grazie

Plate 55. Beatrice d'Este, in the *Crucifixion* by Montorfano, Milan, Santa Maria delle Grazie

Plate 56. Cartoon for a portrait of Isabella d'Este, Paris, Louvre

Plate 57. Cartoon for a *St Anne, Virgin and Child*, London, Royal Academy

Plate 58. *Detail of plate 57*

Plate 59. *Detail of plate 57*

Plate 60. *Detail of plate 57.*

Plate 61. *Detail of plate 57*

Plate 62. MONA LISA, Paris, Louvre

Plate 63. *Detail of plate 62*

Plate 64. *Detail of plate 62*

MONA LISA, Paris, Louvre. (*Detail of plate 62*)

Plate 65. *Detail of plate 62*

Plate 66. ST ANNE, VIRGIN AND CHILD, Paris, Louvre

Plate 67. *Detail of plate 66*

Plate 68. *Detail of plate 66*

Plate 69. *Detail of plate 66*

Plate 70. *Detail of plate 66*

Plate 71. *Detail of plate 66*

Plate 72. ST JOHN THE BAPTIST, Paris, Louvre

Plate 73. *Detail of plate 72*

Plate 74. NURSING MADONNA (MADONNA LITTA), Leningrad,
The Hermitage (*attrib*.)

Plate 75. *Detail of plate 74*

Plate 76. LADY WITH AN ERMINE, Cracow, Czartoryski Museum
(*attrib.*)

Plate 77. LA BELLE FERRONIERE, Paris, Louvre (*attrib.*)

Plate 78. PORTRAIT OF A MUSICIAN, Milan, Pinacoteca Ambrosiana
(*attrib.*)

Plate 79. PORTRAIT OF A LADY, Milan, Pinacoteca Ambrosiana
(*attrib.*)

Plate 80. *Detail of plate 78*

Plate 81. *Detail of plate 77*

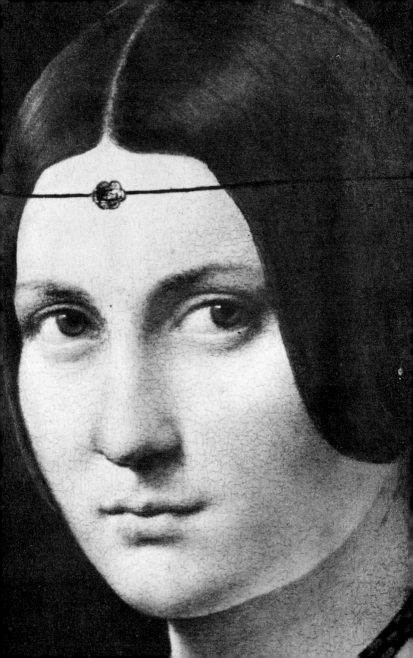

Plate 82. BACCHUS, Paris, Louvre (*attrib.*)

Plate 83. LEDA, Rome, Spiridon Collection (*attrib.*)

Plate 84. Study for *Leda*, Windsor, Royal Library

Plate 85. HEAD OF A YOUNG WOMAN (*attrib.*)

Plate 86. Anonymous: copy of *The Battle of Anghiari*, Florence, Uffizi

Plate 87. Rubens: copy of *The Battle of Anghiari*, Paris, Louvre

Plate 88. Study for *The Battle of Anghiari*, Budapest, Fine Arts Museum

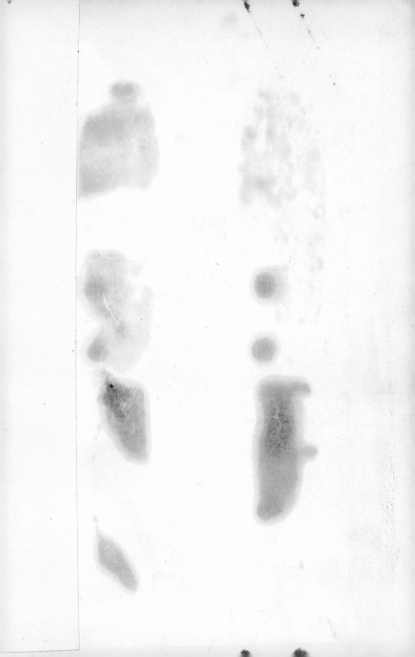

ᴅ
623
L5
323